Poems

By

Ralph Waldo Emerson

Double9
BOOKS

Poems
by Ralph Waldo Emerson

ISBN: 978-93-60463-10-6
Published by

DOUBLE 9 BOOKS

2/13-B, Ansari Road
Daryaganj, New Delhi – 110002
info@double9books.com
www.double9books.com
Tel. 011-40042856

ABOUT THE AUTHOR

Ralph Waldo Emerson was an American essayist, speaker, philosopher, abolitionist, and poet who lived from May 25, 1803 to April 27, 1882. He went by his middle name, Waldo. He led the transcendentalist movement in the middle of the 1800s. People looked up to him as a supporter of freedom and critical thinking, as well as a wise critic of how society and conformity can make people feel bad about themselves. He was called "the most gifted of the Americans" by Friedrich Nietzsche, and Walt Whitman called him his "master." Emerson slowly moved away from the religious and social beliefs of his time. In his 1836 essay "Nature," he formulated and explained the theory of transcendentalism. After this, in 1837, he gave a speech called "The American Scholar." Oliver Wendell Holmes Sr. thought it was America's "intellectual Declaration of Independence." Emerson was born on May 25, 1803, in Newbury, Massachusetts. His parents were Ruth Haskins and the Rev. William Emerson, who was a Unitarian preacher. He was named for Ralph, his mom brother, and Rebecca Waldo, his dad great-grandmother. William, Edward, Robert Bulkeley, and Charles were the other four sons who lived to adulthood. Ralph Waldo was the second of these boys to do so.

CONTENTS

II
MAY-DAY AND OTHER PIECES

III
ELEMENTS AND MOTTOES

V
APPENDIX

VI
POEMS OF YOUTH AND EARLY MANHOOD

PREFACE

In Mr. Cabot's prefatory note to the Riverside Edition of the Poems, published the year after Mr. Emerson's death, he said:—

"This volume contains nearly all the pieces included in the POEMS and MAY-DAY of former editions. In 1876, Mr. Emerson published a selection from his Poems, adding six new ones and omitting many[1] of those omitted, several are now restored, in accordance with the expressed wishes of many readers and lovers of them. Also some pieces never before published are here given in an Appendix; on various grounds. Some of them appear to have had Mr. Emerson's approval, but to have been withheld because they were unfinished. These it seemed best not to suppress, now that they can never receive their completion. Others, mostly of an early date, remained unpublished, doubtless because of their personal and private nature. Some of these seem to have an autobiographic interest sufficient to justify their publication. Others again, often mere fragments, have been admitted as characteristic, or as expressing in poetic form thoughts found in the Essays.

[1]: Little Classic Edition.

"In coming to a decision in these cases it seemed, on the whole, preferable to take the risk of including too much rather than the opposite, and to leave the task of further winnowing to the hands of Time.

"As was stated in the preface to the first volume of this edition of Mr. Emerson's writings, the readings adopted by him in the Selected Poems have not always been followed here, but in some cases preference has been given to corrections made by him when he was in fuller strength than at the time of the last revision.

"A change in the arrangement of the stanzas of 'May-Day,' in the part representative of the march of Spring, received his sanction as bringing them more nearly in accordance with the events in Nature."

In the preparation of the Riverside Edition of the *Poems*, Mr. Cabot very considerately took the present editor into counsel (as representing Mr. Emerson's family), who at that time in turn took counsel with several persons of taste and mature judgment with regard especially to the admission of poems hitherto unpublished and of fragments that seemed interested and pleasing. Mr. Cabot and he were entirely in accord with regard to the Riverside Edition. In the present edition, the substance of the Riverside Edition has been preserved, with hardly an exception, although some poems and fragments have been added. None of the poems therein printed have been omitted. "The House," which appeared in the first volume of *Poems*, and "Nemesis," "Una," "Love and Thought" and "Merlin's Songs," from the *May-Day* volume, have been restored. To the few mottoes of the Essays, which Mr. Emerson printed as "Elements" in *May-Day*, most of the others have been added. Following Mr. Emerson's precedent of giving his brother Edward's "Last Farewell" a place beside the poem in his memory, two pleasing poems by Ellen Tucker, his first wife, which he published in the *Dial*, have been placed with his own poems relating to her. The publication in the last edition of some poems that Mr. Emerson had long kept by him, but had never quite been ready to print, and of various fragments on Poetry, Nature and Life, was not done without advice and careful consideration, and then was felt to be perhaps a rash experiment. The continued interest which has been shown in the author's thought and methods and life—for these unfinished pieces contain much autobiography—has made the present editor feel it justifiable to keep almost all of these and to add a few. Their order has been slightly altered.

A few poems from the verse-books sufficiently complete to have a title are printed in the Appendix for the first time: "Insight," "September," "October," "Hymn" and "Riches."

After much hesitation the editor has gathered in their order of time, and printed at the end of the book, some twenty early pieces, a few of them taken from the Appendix of the last edition and others never printed before. They are for the most part journals in verse covering the period of his school-teaching, study for the ministry and exercise of that office, his sickness, bereavement, travel abroad and return to the new life. This sad period of probation is illuminated by the episode of his first love. Not for their poetical merit, except in flashes, but for the light they throw on the growth of his thought and character are they included.

In this volume the course of the Muse, as Emerson tells it, is pursued with regard to his own poems.

> I hang my verses in the wind,
>
> Time and tide their faults will find.

EDWARD W. EMERSON.

March 12, 1904.

BIOGRAPHICAL SKETCH

The Emersons first appeared in the north of England, but Thomas, who landed in Massachusetts in 1638, came from Hertfordshire. He built soon after a house, sometimes railed the Saint's Rest, which still stands in Ipswich on the slope of Heart-break Hill, close by Labour-in-vain Creek. Ralph Waldo Emerson was the sixth in descent from him. He was born in Boston, in Summer Street, May 25, 1803. He was the third son of William Emerson, the minister of the First Church in Boston, whose father, William Emerson, had been the patriotic minister of Concord at the outbreak of the Revolution, and died a chaplain in the army. Ruth Haskins, the mother of Ralph Waldo Emerson, was left a widow in 1811, with a family of five little boys. The taste of these boys was scholarly, and four of them went through the Latin School to Harvard College, and graduated there. Their mother was a person of great sweetness, dignity, and piety, bringing up her sons wisely and well in very straitened circumstances, and loved by them. Her husband's stepfather, Rev. Dr. Ripley of Concord, helped her, and constantly invited the boys to the Old Manse, so that the woods and fields along the Concord River were first a playground and then the background of the dreams of their awakening imaginations.

Born in the city, Emerson's young mind first found delight in poems and classic prose, to which his instincts led him as naturally as another boy's would to go fishing, but his vacations in the country supplemented these by giving him great and increasing love of nature. In his early poems classic imagery is woven into pictures of New England woodlands. Even as a little boy he had the habit of attempting flights of verse, stimulated by Milton, Pope, or Scott, and he and his mates took pleasure in declaiming to each other in barns and attics. He was so full of thoughts and fancies that he sought the pen instinctively, to jot them down.

At college Emerson did not shine as a scholar, though he won prizes for essays and declamations, being especially unfitted for mathematical studies, and enjoying the classics rather in a literary than grammatical way. And yet it is doubtful whether any man in his class used his time to better purpose with reference to his after life, for young Emerson's instinct led him to wide reading of works, outside the curriculum, that spoke directly to him. He had already formed the habit of writing in a journal, not the facts but the thoughts and inspirations of the day; often, also, good stories or poetical quotations, and scraps of his own verse.

On graduation from Harvard in the class of 1821, following the traditions of his family, Emerson resolved to study to be a minister, and meantime helped his older brother William in the support of the family by teaching in a school for young ladies in Boston, that the former had successfully established. The principal was twenty-one and the assistant nineteen years of age. For school-teaching on the usual lines Emerson was not fitted, and his youth and shyness prevented him from imparting his best gifts to his scholars. Years later, when, in his age, his old scholars assembled to greet him, he regretted that no hint had been brought into the school of what at that very time "I was writing every night in my chamber, my first thoughts on morals and the beautiful laws of compensation, and of individual genius, which to observe and illustrate have given sweetness to many years of my life." Yet many scholars remembered his presence and teaching with pleasure and gratitude, not only in Boston, but in Chelmsford and Roxbury, for while his younger brothers were in college it was necessary that he should help. In these years, as through all his youth, he was loved, spurred on in his intellectual life, and keenly criticised by his aunt, Mary Moody Emerson, an eager and wide reader, inspired by religious zeal, high-minded, but eccentric.

The health of the young teacher suffered from too ascetic a life, and unmistakable danger-signals began to appear, fortunately heeded in time, but disappointment and delay resulted, borne, however, with sense and courage. His course at the Divinity School in Cambridge was much broken; nevertheless, in October, 1826, he was "approbated to preach" by the Middlesex Association of Ministers. A winter at the North at this time threatened to prove fatal, so he was sent South by his helpful kinsman, Rev. Samuel Ripley, and passed the winter in Florida with benefit, working northward in the spring, preaching in the cities, and resumed his studies at Cambridge.

In 1829, Emerson was called by the Second or Old North Church in Boston to become the associate pastor with Rev. Henry Ware, and soon after, because of his senior's delicate health, was called on to assume the full duty. Theological dogmas, such as the Unitarian Church of Channing's day accepted, did not appeal to Emerson, nor did the supernatural in religion in its ordinary acceptation interest him. The omnipresence of spirit, the dignity of man, the daily miracle of the universe, were what he taught, and while the older members of the congregation may have been disquieted that he did not dwell on revealed religion, his words reached the young people, stirred thought, and awakened aspiration. At this time he lived with his mother and his young wife (Ellen Tucker) in Chardon Street. For three years he ministered to his people in Boston. Then having felt the shock of being obliged to conform to church usage, as stated prayer when the spirit did not move, and especially the administration of the Communion, he honestly laid his troubles before his people, and proposed to them some modification of this rite. While they considered his proposition, Emerson went into the White Mountains to weigh his conflicting duties to his church and conscience. He came down, bravely to meet the refusal of the church to change the rite, and in a sermon preached in September, 1832, explained his objections to it, and, because he could not honestly administer it, resigned.

He parted from his people in all kindness, but the wrench was felt. His wife had recently died, he was ill himself, his life seemed to others broken up. But meantime voices from far away had reached him. He sailed for Europe, landed in Italy, saw cities, and art, and men, but would not stay long. Of the dead, Michael Angelo appealed chiefly to him there; Landor among the living. He soon passed northward, making little stay in Paris, but sought out Carlyle, then hardly recognized, and living in the lonely hills of the Scottish Border. There began a friendship which had great influence on the lives of both men, and lasted through life. He also visited Wordsworth. But the new life before him called him home.

He landed at Boston within the year in good health and hope, and joined his mother and youngest brother Charles in Newton. Frequent invitations to preach still came, and were accepted, and he even was sounded as to succeeding Dr. Dewey in the church at New Bedford; but, as he stipulated for freedom from ceremonial, this came to nothing.

In the autumn of 1834 he moved to Concord, living with his kinsman, Dr. Ripley, at the Manse, but soon bought house and land on the Boston Road, on the edge of the village towards Walden woods. Thither, in the autumn, he brought his wife. Miss Lidian Jackson, of Plymouth, and this was their home during the rest of their lives.

The new life to which he had been called opened pleasantly and increased in happiness and opportunity, except for the sadness of bereavements, for, in the first few years, his brilliant brothers Edward and Charles died, and soon afterward Waldo, his firstborn son, and later his mother. Emerson had left traditional religion, the city, the Old World, behind, and now went to Nature as his teacher, his inspiration. His first book, "Nature," which he was meditating while in Europe, was finished here, and published in 1836. His practice during all his life in Concord was to go alone to the woods almost daily, sometimes to wait there for hours, and, when thus attuned, to receive the message to which he was to give voice. Though it might be colored by him in transmission, he held that the light was universal.

"Ever the words of the Gods resound,

But the porches of man's ear

Seldom in this low life's round

Are unsealed that he may hear."

But he resorted, also, to the books of those who had handed down the oracles truly, and was quick to find the message destined for him. Men, too, he studied eagerly, the humblest and the highest, regretting always that the brand of the scholar on him often silenced the men of shop and office where he came. He was everywhere a learner, expecting light from the youngest and least educated visitor. The thoughts combined with the flower of his reading were gradually grouped into lectures, and his main occupation through life was reading these to who would hear, at first in courses in Boston, but later all over the country, for the Lyceum sprang up in New England in these years in every town, and spread westward to the new settlements even beyond the Mississippi. His winters were spent in these rough, but to him interesting journeys, for he loved to watch the growth of the Republic in which he had faith, and his summers were spent in study and writing. These lectures were later severely pruned and revised, and the best of them gathered into seven volumes of essays under different names between 1841 and 1876. The courses in Boston, which at first were given in the Masonic Temple, were always well attended by earnest and thoughtful people. The young, whether in years or in spirit, were always and to the end his audience of the spoken or written word. The freedom of the Lyceum platform pleased Emerson. He found that people would hear on Wednesday with approval and unsuspectingly doctrines from which on Sunday they felt officially obliged to dissent.

Mr. Lowell, in his essays, has spoken of these early lectures and what they were worth to him and others suffering from the generous discontent of youth with things as they were. Emerson used to say, "My strength and my doom is to be solitary;" but to a retired scholar a wholesome offset to this was the travelling and lecturing in cities and in raw frontier towns, bringing him into touch with the people, and this he knew and valued.

In 1837 Emerson gave the Phi Beta Kappa oration in Cambridge, The American Scholar, which increased his growing reputation, but the following year his Address to the Senior Class at the Divinity School brought out, even from the friendly Unitarians, severe strictures and warnings against its dangerous doctrines. Of this heresy Emerson said: "I deny personality to God because it is too little, not too much." He really strove to elevate the idea of God. Yet those who were pained or shocked by his teachings respected Emerson. His lectures were still in demand; he was often asked to speak by literary societies at orthodox colleges. He preached regularly at East Lexington until 1838, but thereafter withdrew from the ministerial office. At this time the progressive and spiritually minded young people used to meet for discussion and help in Boston, among them George Ripley, Cyrus Bartol, James Freeman Clarke, Alcott, Dr. Hedge, Margaret Fuller, and Elizabeth Peabody. Perhaps from this gathering of friends, which Emerson attended, came what is called the Transcendental Movement, two results of which were the Brook Farm Community and the Dial magazine, in which last Emerson took great interest, and was for the time an editor. Many of these friends were frequent visitors in Concord. Alcott moved thither after the breaking up of his school. Hawthorne also came to dwell there. Henry Thoreau, a Concord youth, greatly interested Emerson; indeed, became for a year or two a valued inmate of his home, and helped and instructed him in the labors of the garden and little farm, which gradually grew to ten acres, the chief interest of which for the owner was his trees, which he loved and tended. Emerson helped introduce his countrymen to the teachings of Carlyle, and edited his works here, where they found more readers than at home.

In 1847 Emerson was invited to read lectures in England, and remained abroad a year, visiting France also in her troublous times. English Traits was a result. Just before this journey he had collected and published his poems. A later volume, called May Day, followed in 1867. He had written verses from childhood, and to the purified expression of poetry he, through life, eagerly aspired. He said, "I like my poems best because it is not I who write them." In 1866 the degree of Doctor of Laws was conferred on him by Harvard University, and he was chosen an Overseer. In 1867 he again gave the Phi Beta Kappa oration, and in 1870 and 1871 gave courses in Philosophy in the University Lectures at Cambridge.

Emerson was not merely a man of letters. He recognized and did the private and public duties of the hour. He exercised a wide hospitality to souls as well as bodies. Eager youths came to him for rules, and went away with light. Reformers, wise and unwise, came to him, and were kindly received. They were often disappointed that they could not harness him to their partial and transient scheme. He said, My reforms include theirs: I must go my way; help people by my strength, not by my weakness. But if a storm threatened, he felt bound to appear and show his colors. Against the crying evils of his time he worked bravely in his own way. He wrote to President Van Buren against the wrong done to the Cherokees, dared speak against the idolized Webster, when he deserted the cause of Freedom, constantly spoke of the iniquity of slavery, aided with speech and money the Free State cause in Kansas, was at Phillips's side at the antislavery meeting in 1861 broken up by the Boston mob, urged emancipation during the war.

He enjoyed his Concord home and neighbors, served on the school committee for years, did much for the Lyceum, and spoke on the town's great occasions. He went to all town-meetings, oftener to listen and admire than to speak, and always took pleasure and pride in the people. In return he was respected and loved by them.

Emerson's house was destroyed by fire in 1872, and the incident exposure and fatigue did him harm. His many friends insisted on rebuilding his house and sending him abroad to get well. He went up the Nile, and revisited England, finding old and new friends, and, on his return, was welcomed and escorted home by the people of Concord. After this time he was unable to write. His old age was quiet and happy among his family and friends. He died in April, 1882.

EDWARD W. EMERSON.

January, 1899.

I
POEMS

GOOD-BYE

Good-bye, proud world! I'm going home:
Thou art not my friend, and I'm not thine.
Long through thy weary crowds I roam;
A river-ark on the ocean brine,
Long I've been tossed like the driven foam:
But now, proud world! I'm going home.

Good-bye to Flattery's fawning face;
To Grandeur with his wise grimace;
To upstart Wealth's averted eye;
To supple Office, low and high;
To crowded halls, to court and street;
To frozen hearts and hasting feet;
To those who go, and those who come;
Good-bye, proud world! I'm going home.

I am going to my own hearth-stone,
Bosomed in yon green hills alone,—
secret nook in a pleasant land,
Whose groves the frolic fairies planned;
Where arches green, the livelong day,
Echo the blackbird's roundelay,
And vulgar feet have never trod
A spot that is sacred to thought and God.

O, when I am safe in my sylvan home,
I tread on the pride of Greece and Rome;
And when I am stretched beneath the pines,
Where the evening star so holy shines,
I laugh at the lore and the pride of man,
At the sophist schools and the learned clan;
For what are they all, in their high conceit,
When man in the bush with God may meet?

EACH AND ALL

Little thinks, in the field, yon red-cloaked clown
Of thee from the hill-top looking down;
The heifer that lows in the upland farm,
Far-heard, lows not thine ear to charm;
The sexton, tolling his bell at noon,
Deems not that great Napoleon
Stops his horse, and lists with delight,
Whilst his files sweep round yon Alpine height;
Nor knowest thou what argument
Thy life to thy neighbor's creed has lent.
All are needed by each one;
Nothing is fair or good alone.
I thought the sparrow's note from heaven,
Singing at dawn on the alder bough;
I brought him home, in his nest, at even;
He sings the song, but it cheers not now,
For I did not bring home the river and sky; —
He sang to my ear, — they sang to my eye.
The delicate shells lay on the shore;
The bubbles of the latest wave
Fresh pearls to their enamel gave,
And the bellowing of the savage sea
Greeted their safe escape to me.
I wiped away the weeds and foam,
I fetched my sea-born treasures home;
But the poor, unsightly, noisome things
Had left their beauty on the shore
With the sun and the sand and the wild uproar.

The lover watched his graceful maid,
As 'mid the virgin train she strayed,
Nor knew her beauty's best attire
Was woven still by the snow-white choir.
At last she came to his hermitage,
Like the bird from the woodlands to the cage;—
The gay enchantment was undone,
A gentle wife, but fairy none.
Then I said, 'I covet truth;
Beauty is unripe childhood's cheat;
I leave it behind with the games of youth:'—
As I spoke, beneath my feet
The ground-pine curled its pretty wreath,
Running over the club-moss burrs;
I inhaled the violet's breath;
Around me stood the oaks and firs;
Pine-cones and acorns lay on the ground;
Over me soared the eternal sky.
Full of light and of deity;
Again I saw, again I heard,
The rolling river, the morning bird;—
Beauty through my senses stole;
I yielded myself to the perfect whole.

THE PROBLEM

I like a church; I like a cowl;
I love a prophet of the soul;
And on my heart monastic aisles
Fall like sweet strains, or pensive smiles
Yet not for all his faith can see
Would I that cowlèd churchman be.

Why should the vest on him allure,
Which I could not on me endure?

Not from a vain or shallow thought
His awful Jove young Phidias brought;
Never from lips of cunning fell
The thrilling Delphic oracle;
Out from the heart of nature rolled
The burdens of the Bible old;
The litanies of nations came,
Like the volcano's tongue of flame,
Up from the burning core below,—
The canticles of love and woe:
The hand that rounded Peter's dome
And groined the aisles of Christian Rome
Wrought in a sad sincerity;
Himself from God he could not free;
He builded better than he knew;—
The conscious stone to beauty grew.

Know'st thou what wove yon woodbird's nest
Of leaves, and feathers from her breast?

Or how the fish outbuilt her shell,
Painting with morn each annual cell?
Or how the sacred pine-tree adds
To her old leaves new myriads?
Such and so grew these holy piles,
Whilst love and terror laid the tiles.
Earth proudly wears the Parthenon,
As the best gem upon her zone,
And Morning opes with haste her lids
To gaze upon the Pyramids;
O'er England's abbeys bends the sky,
As on its friends, with kindred eye;
For out of Thought's interior sphere
These wonders rose to upper air;
And Nature gladly gave them place,
Adopted them into her race,
And granted them an equal date
With Andes and with Ararat.

These temples grew as grows the grass;
Art might obey, but not surpass.
The passive Master lent his hand
To the vast soul that o'er him planned;
And the same power that reared the shrine
Bestrode the tribes that knelt within.
Ever the fiery Pentecost
Girds with one flame the countless host,
Trances the heart through chanting choirs,
And through the priest the mind inspires.
The word unto the prophet spoken
Was writ on tables yet unbroken;
The word by seers or sibyls told,
In groves of oak, or fanes of gold,
Still floats upon the morning wind,
Still whispers to the willing mind.

One accent of the Holy Ghost
The heedless world hath never lost.
I know what say the fathers wise, —
The Book itself before me lies,
Old *Chrysostom,* best Augustine,
And he who blent both in his line,
The younger *Golden Lips* or mines,
Taylor, the Shakspeare of divines.
His words are music in my ear,
I see his cowlèd portrait dear;
And yet, for all his faith could see,
I would not the good bishop be.

TO RHEA

Thee, dear friend, a brother soothes,
Not with flatteries, but truths,
Which tarnish not, but purify
To light which dims the morning's eye.
I have come from the spring-woods,
From the fragrant solitudes;—
Listen what the poplar-tree
And murmuring waters counselled me.

If with love thy heart has burned;
If thy love is unreturned;
Hide thy grief within thy breast,
Though it tear thee unexpressed;
For when love has once departed
From the eyes of the false-hearted,
And one by one has torn off quite
The bandages of purple light;
Though thou wert the loveliest
Form the soul had ever dressed,
Thou shalt seem, in each reply,
A vixen to his altered eye;
Thy softest pleadings seem too bold,
Thy praying lute will seem to scold;
Though thou kept the straightest road,
Yet thou errest far and broad.

But thou shalt do as do the gods
In their cloudless periods;
For of this lore be thou sure,—

Though thou forget, the gods, secure,
Forget never their command,
But make the statute of this land.
As they lead, so follow all,
Ever have done, ever shall.
Warning to the blind and deaf,
'T is written on the iron leaf,
Who drinks of Cupid's nectar cup
Loveth downward, and not up;
He who loves, of gods or men,
Shall not by the same be loved again;
His sweetheart's idolatry
Falls, in turn, a new degree.
When a god is once beguiled
By beauty of a mortal child
And by her radiant youth delighted,
He is not fooled, but warily knoweth
His love shall never be requited.
And thus the wise Immortal doeth,—
'T is his study and delight
To bless that creature day and night;
From all evils to defend her;
In her lap to pour all splendor;
To ransack earth for riches rare,
And fetch her stars to deck her hair:
He mixes music with her thoughts,
And saddens her with heavenly doubts:
All grace, all good his great heart knows,
Profuse in love, the king bestows,
Saying, 'Hearken! Earth, Sea, Air!
This monument of my despair
Build I to the All-Good, All-Fair.
Not for a private good,
But I, from my beatitude,

Albeit scorned as none was scorned,
Adorn her as was none adorned.
I make this maiden an ensample
To Nature, through her kingdoms ample,
Whereby to model newer races,
Statelier forms and fairer faces;
To carry man to new degrees
Of power and of comeliness.
These presents be the hostages
Which I pawn for my release.
See to thyself, O Universe!
Thou art better, and not worse.' —
And the god, having given all,
Is freed forever from his thrall.

THE VISIT

Askest, 'How long thou shalt stay?'
Devastator of the day!
Know, each substance and relation,
Thorough nature's operation,
Hath its unit, bound and metre;
And every new compound
Is some product and repeater,—
Product of the earlier found.
But the unit of the visit,
The encounter of the wise,—
Say, what other metre is it
Than the meeting of the eyes?
Nature poureth into nature
Through the channels of that feature,
Riding on the ray of sight,
Fleeter far than whirlwinds go,
Or for service, or delight,
Hearts to hearts their meaning show,
Sum their long experience,
And import intelligence.
Single look has drained the breast;
Single moment years confessed.
The duration of a glance
Is the term of convenance,
And, though thy rede be church or state,
Frugal multiples of that.
Speeding Saturn cannot halt;
Linger,—thou shalt rue the fault:
If Love his moment overstay,
Hatred's swift repulsions play.

URIEL

It fell in the ancient periods
Which the brooding soul surveys,
Or ever the wild Time coined itself
Into calendar months and days.

This was the lapse of Uriel,
Which in Paradise befell.
Once, among the Pleiads walking,
Seyd overheard the young gods talking;
And the treason, too long pent,
To his ears was evident.
The young deities discussed
Laws of form, and metre just,
Orb, quintessence, and sunbeams,
What subsisteth, and what seems.
One, with low tones that decide,
And doubt and reverend use defied,
With a look that solved the sphere,
And stirred the devils everywhere,
Gave his sentiment divine
Against the being of a line.
'Line in nature is not found;
Unit and universe are round;
In vain produced, all rays return;
Evil will bless, and ice will burn.'
As Uriel spoke with piercing eye,
A shudder ran around the sky;
The stern old war-gods shook their heads,

The seraphs frowned from myrtle-beds;
Seemed to the holy festival
The rash word boded ill to all;
The balance-beam of Fate was bent;
The bounds of good and ill were rent;
Strong Hades could not keep his own,
But all slid to confusion.

A sad self-knowledge, withering, fell
On the beauty of Uriel;
In heaven once eminent, the god
Withdrew, that hour, into his cloud;
Whether doomed to long gyration
In the sea of generation,
Or by knowledge grown too bright
To hit the nerve of feebler sight.
Straightway, a forgetting wind
Stole over the celestial kind,
And their lips the secret kept,
If in ashes the fire-seed slept.
But now and then, truth-speaking things
Shamed the angels' veiling wings;
And, shrilling from the solar course,
Or from fruit of chemic force,
Procession of a soul in matter,
Or the speeding change of water,
Or out of the good of evil born,
Came Uriel's voice of cherub scorn,
And a blush tinged the upper sky,
And the gods shook, they knew not why.

THE WORLD-SOUL

Thanks to the morning light,
Thanks to the foaming sea,
To the uplands of New Hampshire,
To the green-haired forest free;
Thanks to each man of courage,
To the maids of holy mind,
To the boy with his games undaunted
Who never looks behind.

Cities of proud hotels,
Houses of rich and great,
Vice nestles in your chambers,
Beneath your roofs of slate.
It cannot conquer folly,—
Time-and-space-conquering steam,—
And the light-outspeeding telegraph
Bears nothing on its beam.

The politics are base;
The letters do not cheer;
And 'tis far in the deeps of history,
The voice that speaketh clear.
Trade and the streets ensnare us,
Our bodies are weak and worn;
We plot and corrupt each other,
And we despoil the unborn.

Yet there in the parlor sits
Some figure of noble guise,—

Our angel, in a stranger's form,
Or woman's pleading eyes;
Or only a flashing sunbeam
In at the window-pane;
Or Music pours on mortals
Its beautiful disdain.

The inevitable morning
Finds them who in cellars be;
And be sure the all-loving Nature
Will smile in a factory.
Yon ridge of purple landscape,
Yon sky between the walls,
Hold all the hidden wonders
In scanty intervals.

Alas! the Sprite that haunts us
Deceives our rash desire;
It whispers of the glorious gods,
And leaves us in the mire.
We cannot learn the cipher
That's writ upon our cell;
Stars taunt us by a mystery
Which we could never spell.

If but one hero knew it,
The world would blush in flame;
The sage, till he hit the secret,
Would hang his head for shame.
Our brothers have not read it,
Not one has found the key;
And henceforth we are comforted, —
We are but such as they.

Still, still the secret presses;
The nearing clouds draw down;

The crimson morning flames into
The fopperies of the town.
Within, without the idle earth,
Stars weave eternal rings;
The sun himself shines heartily,
And shares the joy he brings.

And what if Trade sow cities
Like shells along the shore,
And thatch with towns the prairie broad
With railways ironed o'er? —
They are but sailing foam-bells
Along Thought's causing stream,
And take their shape and sun-color
From him that sends the dream.

For Destiny never swerves
Nor yields to men the helm;
He shoots his thought, by hidden nerves,
Throughout the solid realm.
The patient Daemon sits,
With roses and a shroud;
He has his way, and deals his gifts, —
But ours is not allowed.

He is no churl nor trifler,
And his viceroy is none, —
Love-without-weakness, —
Of Genius sire and son.
And his will is not thwarted;
The seeds of land and sea
Are the atoms of his body bright,
And his behest obey.

He serveth the servant,
The brave he loves amain;

He kills the cripple and the sick,
And straight begins again;
For gods delight in gods,
And thrust the weak aside;
To him who scorns their charities
Their arms fly open wide.

When the old world is sterile
And the ages are effete,
He will from wrecks and sediment
The fairer world complete.
He forbids to despair;
His cheeks mantle with mirth;
And the unimagined good of men
Is yeaning at the birth.

Spring still makes spring in the mind
When sixty years are told;
Love wakes anew this throbbing heart,
And we are never old;
Over the winter glaciers
I see the summer glow,
And through the wild-piled snow-drift
The warm rosebuds below.

THE SPHINX

The Sphinx is drowsy,
Her wings are furled:
Her ear is heavy,
She broods on the world.
"Who'll tell me my secret,
The ages have kept?—
I awaited the seer
While they slumbered and slept:—

"The fate of the man-child,
The meaning of man;
Known fruit of the unknown;
Daedalian plan;
Out of sleeping a waking,
Out of waking a sleep;
Life death overtaking;
Deep underneath deep?

"Erect as a sunbeam,
Upspringeth the palm;
The elephant browses,
Undaunted and calm;
In beautiful motion
The thrush plies his wings;
Kind leaves of his covert,
Your silence he sings.

"The waves, unashamèd,
In difference sweet,

Play glad with the breezes,
Old playfellows meet;
The journeying atoms,
Primordial wholes,
Firmly draw, firmly drive,
By their animate poles.

"Sea, earth, air, sound, silence.
Plant, quadruped, bird,
By one music enchanted,
One deity stirred, —
Each the other adorning,
Accompany still;
Night veileth the morning,
The vapor the hill.

"The babe by its mother
Lies bathèd in joy;
Glide its hours uncounted, —
The sun is its toy;
Shines the peace of all being,
Without cloud, in its eyes;
And the sum of the world
In soft miniature lies.

"But man crouches and blushes,
Absconds and conceals;
He creepeth and peepeth,
He palters and steals;
Infirm, melancholy,
Jealous glancing around,
An oaf, an accomplice,
He poisons the ground.

"Out spoke the great mother,
Beholding his fear; —

At the sound of her accents
Cold shuddered the sphere:—
'Who has drugged my boy's cup?
Who has mixed my boy's bread?
Who, with sadness and madness,
Has turned my child's head?'"

I heard a poet answer
Aloud and cheerfully,
'Say on, sweet Sphinx! thy dirges
Are pleasant songs to me.
Deep love lieth under
These pictures of time;
They fade in the light of
Their meaning sublime.

"The fiend that man harries
Is love of the Best;
Yawns the pit of the Dragon,
Lit by rays from the Blest.
The Lethe of Nature
Can't trance him again,
Whose soul sees the perfect,
Which his eyes seek in vain.

"To vision profounder,
Man's spirit must dive;
His aye-rolling orb
At no goal will arrive;
The heavens that now draw him
With sweetness untold,
Once found,—for new heavens
He spurneth the old.

"Pride ruined the angels,
Their shame them restores;

Lurks the joy that is sweetest
In stings of remorse.
Have I a lover
Who is noble and free?—
I would he were nobler
Than to love me.

"Eterne alternation
Now follows, now flies;
And under pain, pleasure,—
Under pleasure, pain lies.
Love works at the centre,
Heart-heaving alway;
Forth speed the strong pulses
To the borders of day.

"Dull Sphinx, Jove keep thy five wits;
Thy sight is growing blear;
Rue, myrrh and cummin for the Sphinx,
Her muddy eyes to clear!"
The old Sphinx bit her thick lip,—
Said, "Who taught thee me to name?
I am thy spirit, yoke-fellow;
Of thine eye I am eyebeam.

"Thou art the unanswered question;
Couldst see thy proper eye,
Alway it asketh, asketh;
And each answer is a lie.
So take thy quest through nature,
It through thousand natures ply;
Ask on, thou clothed eternity;
Time is the false reply."

Uprose the merry Sphinx,
And crouched no more in stone;

She melted into purple cloud,
She silvered in the moon;
She spired into a yellow flame;
She flowered in blossoms red;
She flowed into a foaming wave:
She stood Monadnoc's head.

Thorough a thousand voices
Spoke the universal dame;
"Who telleth one of my meanings
Is master of all I am."

ALPHONSO OF CASTILE

I, Alphonso, live and learn,
Seeing Nature go astern.
Things deteriorate in kind;
Lemons run to leaves and rind;
Meagre crop of figs and limes;
Shorter days and harder times.
Flowering April cools and dies
In the insufficient skies.
Imps, at high midsummer, blot
Half the sun's disk with a spot;
'Twill not now avail to tan
Orange cheek or skin of man.
Roses bleach, the goats are dry,
Lisbon quakes, the people cry.
Yon pale, scrawny fisher fools,
Gaunt as bitterns in the pools,
Are no brothers of my blood;—
They discredit Adamhood.
Eyes of gods! ye must have seen,
O'er your ramparts as ye lean,
The general debility;
Of genius the sterility;
Mighty projects countermanded;
Rash ambition, brokenhanded;
Puny man and scentless rose
Tormenting Pan to double the dose.
Rebuild or ruin: either fill
Of vital force the wasted rill,

Or tumble all again in heap
To weltering Chaos and to sleep.

Say, Seigniors, are the old Niles dry,
Which fed the veins of earth and sky,
That mortals miss the loyal heats,
Which drove them erst to social feats;
Now, to a savage selfness grown,
Think nature barely serves for one;
With science poorly mask their hurt;
And vex the gods with question pert,
Immensely curious whether you
Still are rulers, or Mildew?

Masters, I'm in pain with you;
Masters, I'll be plain with you;
In my palace of Castile,
I, a king, for kings can feel.
There my thoughts the matter roll,
And solve and oft resolve the whole.
And, for I'm styled Alphonse the Wise,
Ye shall not fail for sound advice.
Before ye want a drop of rain,
Hear the sentiment of Spain.

You have tried famine: no more try it;
Ply us now with a full diet;
Teach your pupils now with plenty,
For one sun supply us twenty.
I have thought it thoroughly over, —
State of hermit, state of lover;
We must have society,
We cannot spare variety.
Hear you, then, celestial fellows!
Fits not to be overzealous;
Steads not to work on the clean jump,

Nor wine nor brains perpetual pump.
Men and gods are too extense;
Could you slacken and condense?
Your rank overgrowths reduce
Till your kinds abound with juice?
Earth, crowded, cries, 'Too many men!'
My counsel is, kill nine in ten,
And bestow the shares of all
On the remnant decimal.
Add their nine lives to this cat;
Stuff their nine brains in one hat;
Make his frame and forces square
With the labors he must dare;
Thatch his flesh, and even his years
With the marble which he rears.
There, growing slowly old at ease
No faster than his planted trees,
He may, by warrant of his age,
In schemes of broader scope engage.
So shall ye have a man of the sphere
Fit to grace the solar year.

MITHRIDATES

I cannot spare water or wine,
Tobacco-leaf, or poppy, or rose;
From the earth-poles to the Line,
All between that works or grows,
Every thing is kin of mine.

Give me agates for my meat;
Give me cantharids to eat;
From air and ocean bring me foods,
From all zones and altitudes;—

From all natures, sharp and slimy,
Salt and basalt, wild and tame:
Tree and lichen, ape, sea-lion,
Bird, and reptile, be my game.

Ivy for my fillet band;
Blinding dog-wood in my hand;
Hemlock for my sherbet cull me,
And the prussic juice to lull me;
Swing me in the upas boughs,
Vampyre-fanned, when I carouse.

Too long shut in strait and few,
Thinly dieted on dew,
I will use the world, and sift it,
To a thousand humors shift it,
As you spin a cherry.
O doleful ghosts, and goblins merry!
O all you virtues, methods, mights,

Means, appliances, delights,
Reputed wrongs and braggart rights,
Smug routine, and things allowed,
Minorities, things under cloud!
Hither! take me, use me, fill me,
Vein and artery, though ye kill me!

TO J.W.

Set not thy foot on graves;
Hear what wine and roses say;
The mountain chase, the summer waves,
The crowded town, thy feet may well delay.

Set not thy foot on graves;
Nor seek to unwind the shroud
Which charitable Time
And Nature have allowed
To wrap the errors of a sage sublime.

Set not thy foot on graves;
Care not to strip the dead
Of his sad ornament,
His myrrh, and wine, and rings,

His sheet of lead,
And trophies buried:
Go, get them where he earned them when alive;
As resolutely dig or dive.

Life is too short to waste
In critic peep or cynic bark,
Quarrel or reprimand:
'T will soon be dark;
Up! mind thine own aim, and
God speed the mark!

DESTINY

That you are fair or wise is vain,
Or strong, or rich, or generous;
You must add the untaught strain
That sheds beauty on the rose.
There's a melody born of melody,
Which melts the world into a sea.
Toil could never compass it;
Art its height could never hit;
It came never out of wit;
But a music music-born
Well may Jove and Juno scorn.
Thy beauty, if it lack the fire
Which drives me mad with sweet desire,
What boots it? What the soldier's mail,
Unless he conquer and prevail?
What all the goods thy pride which lift,
If thou pine for another's gift?
Alas! that one is born in blight,
Victim of perpetual slight:
When thou lookest on his face,
Thy heart saith, 'Brother, go thy ways!
None shall ask thee what thou doest,
Or care a rush for what thou knowest,
Or listen when thou repliest,
Or remember where thou liest,
Or how thy supper is sodden;'
And another is born
To make the sun forgotten.

Surely he carries a talisman
Under his tongue;
Broad his shoulders are and strong;
And his eye is scornful,
Threatening and young.
I hold it of little matter
Whether your jewel be of pure water,
A rose diamond or a white,
But whether it dazzle me with light.
I care not how you are dressed,
In coarsest weeds or in the best;
Nor whether your name is base or brave:
Nor for the fashion of your behavior;
But whether you charm me,
Bid my bread feed and my fire warm me
And dress up Nature in your favor.
One thing is forever good;
That one thing is Success, —
Dear to the Eumenides,
And to all the heavenly brood.
Who bides at home, nor looks abroad,
Carries the eagles, and masters the sword.

GUY

Mortal mixed of middle clay,
Attempered to the night and day,
Interchangeable with things,
Needs no amulets nor rings.
Guy possessed the talisman
That all things from him began;
And as, of old, Polycrates
Chained the sunshine and the breeze,
So did Guy betimes discover
Fortune was his guard and lover;
In strange junctures, felt, with awe,
His own symmetry with law;
That no mixture could withstand
The virtue of his lucky hand.
He gold or jewel could not lose,
Nor not receive his ample dues.
Fearless Guy had never foes,
He did their weapons decompose.
Aimed at him, the blushing blade
Healed as fast the wounds it made.
If on the foeman fell his gaze,
Him it would straightway blind or craze,
In the street, if he turned round,
His eye the eye 't was seeking found.

It seemed his Genius discreet
Worked on the Maker's own receipt,
And made each tide and element

Stewards of stipend and of rent;
So that the common waters fell
As costly wine into his well.
He had so sped his wise affairs
That he caught Nature in his snares.
Early or late, the falling rain
Arrived in time to swell his grain;
Stream could not so perversely wind
But corn of Guy's was there to grind:
The siroc found it on its way,
To speed his sails, to dry his hay;
And the world's sun seemed to rise
To drudge all day for Guy the wise.
In his rich nurseries, timely skill
Strong crab with nobler blood did fill;
The zephyr in his garden rolled
From plum-trees vegetable gold;
And all the hours of the year
With their own harvest honored were.
There was no frost but welcome came,
Nor freshet, nor midsummer flame.
Belonged to wind and world the toil
And venture, and to Guy the oil.

HAMATREYA

Bulkeley, Hunt, Willard, Hosmer, Meriam, Flint,
Possessed the land which rendered to their toil
Hay, corn, roots, hemp, flax, apples, wool and wood.
Each of these landlords walked amidst his farm,
Saying, ''Tis mine, my children's and my name's.
How sweet the west wind sounds in my own trees!
How graceful climb those shadows on my hill!
I fancy these pure waters and the flags
Know me, as does my dog: we sympathize;
And, I affirm, my actions smack of the soil.'

Where are these men? Asleep beneath their grounds:
And strangers, fond as they, their furrows plough.
Earth laughs in flowers, to see her boastful boys
Earth-proud, proud of the earth which is not theirs;
Who steer the plough, but cannot steer their feet
Clear of the grave.
They added ridge to valley, brook to pond,
And sighed for all that bounded their domain;
'This suits me for a pasture; that's my park;
We must have clay, lime, gravel, granite-ledge,
And misty lowland, where to go for peat.
The land is well,—lies fairly to the south.
'Tis good, when you have crossed the sea and back,
To find the sitfast acres where you left them.'
Ah! the hot owner sees not Death, who adds
Him to his land, a lump of mould the more.
Hear what the Earth says:—

EARTH-SONG

'Mine and yours;
Mine, not yours.
Earth endures;
Stars abide—
Shine down in the old sea;
Old are the shores;
But where are old men?
I who have seen much,
Such have I never seen.

'The lawyer's deed
Ran sure,
In tail,
To them, and to their heirs
Who shall succeed,
Without fail,
Forevermore.

'Here is the land,
Shaggy with wood,
With its old valley,
Mound and flood.
But the heritors?—

Fled like the flood's foam.
The lawyer, and the laws,
And the kingdom,
Clean swept herefrom.

'They called me theirs,
Who so controlled me;
Yet every one
Wished to stay, and is gone,
How am I theirs,

If they cannot hold me,
But I hold them?'

When I heard the Earth-song
I was no longer brave;
My avarice cooled
Like lust in the chill of the grave.

THE RHODORA

ON BEING ASKED, WHENCE IS THE FLOWER?

In May, when sea-winds pierced our solitudes,
I found the fresh Rhodora in the woods,
Spreading its leafless blooms in a damp nook,
To please the desert and the sluggish brook.
The purple petals, fallen in the pool,
Made the black water with their beauty gay;
Here might the red-bird come his plumes to cool.
And court the flower that cheapens his array.
Rhodora! if the sages ask thee why
This charm is wasted on the earth and sky,
Tell them, dear, that if eyes were made for seeing,
Then Beauty is its own excuse for being:
Why thou wert there, O rival of the rose!
I never thought to ask, I never knew:
But, in my simple ignorance, suppose
The self-same Power that brought me there brought you.

THE HUMBLE-BEE

Burly, dozing humble-bee,
Where thou art is clime for me.
Let them sail for Porto Rique,
Far-off heats through seas to seek;
I will follow thee alone,
Thou animated torrid-zone!
Zigzag steerer, desert cheerer,
Let me chase thy waving lines;
Keep me nearer, me thy hearer,
Singing over shrubs and vines.

Insect lover of the sun,
Joy of thy dominion!
Sailor of the atmosphere;
Swimmer through the waves of air;
Voyager of light and noon;
Epicurean of June;
Wait, I prithee, till I come
Within earshot of thy hum, —
All without is martyrdom.

When the south wind, in May days,
With a net of shining haze
Silvers the horizon wall,
And with softness touching all,
Tints the human countenance
With a color of romance,
And infusing subtle heats,

Turns the sod to violets,
Thou, in sunny solitudes,
Rover of the underwoods,
The green silence dost displace
With thy mellow, breezy bass.

Hot midsummer's petted crone,
Sweet to me thy drowsy tone
Tells of countless sunny hours,
Long days, and solid banks of flowers;
Of gulfs of sweetness without bound
In Indian wildernesses found;
Of Syrian peace, immortal leisure,
Firmest cheer, and bird-like pleasure.

Aught unsavory or unclean
Hath my insect never seen;
But violets and bilberry bells,
Maple-sap and daffodels,
Grass with green flag half-mast high,
Succory to match the sky,
Columbine with horn of honey,
Scented fern, and agrimony,
Clover, catchfly, adder's-tongue
And brier-roses, dwelt among;
All beside was unknown waste,
All was picture as he passed.

Wiser far than human seer,
Yellow-breeched philosopher!
Seeing only what is fair,
Sipping only what is sweet,
Thou dost mock at fate and care,
Leave the chaff, and take the wheat.

When the fierce northwestern blast
Cools sea and land so far and fast,
Thou already slumberest deep;
Woe and want thou canst outsleep;
Want and woe, which torture us,
Thy sleep makes ridiculous.

BERRYING

'May be true what I had heard, —
Earth's a howling wilderness,
Truculent with fraud and force,'
Said I, strolling through the pastures,
And along the river-side.
Caught among the blackberry vines,
Feeding on the Ethiops sweet,
Pleasant fancies overtook me.
I said, 'What influence me preferred,
Elect, to dreams thus beautiful?'
The vines replied, 'And didst thou deem
No wisdom from our berries went?'

THE SNOW-STORM

Announced by all the trumpets of the sky,
Arrives the snow, and, driving o'er the fields,
Seems nowhere to alight: the whited air
Hides hills and woods, the river, and the heaven,
And veils the farm-house at the garden's end.
The sled and traveller stopped, the courier's feet
Delayed, all friends shut out, the housemates sit
Around the radiant fireplace, enclosed
In a tumultuous privacy of storm.

Come see the north wind's masonry.
Out of an unseen quarry
Furnished with tile, the fierce artificer
Curves his white bastions with projected roof
Round every windward stake, or tree, or door.
Speeding, the myriad-handed, his wild work
So fanciful, so savage, nought cares he
For number or proportion. Mockingly,
On coop or kennel he hangs Parian wreaths;
A swan-like form invests the hidden thorn;
Fills up the farmer's lane from wall to wall,
Maugre the farmer's sighs; and at the gate
A tapering turret overtops the work.
And when his hours are numbered, and the world
Is all his own, retiring, as he were not,
Leaves, when the sun appears, astonished Art
To mimic in slow structures, stone by stone,
Built in an age, the mad wind's night-work,
The frolic architecture of the snow.

WOODNOTES I

1

When the pine tosses its cones
To the song of its waterfall tones,
Who speeds to the woodland walks?
To birds and trees who talks?
Caesar of his leafy Rome,
There the poet is at home.
He goes to the river-side, —
Not hook nor line hath he;
He stands in the meadows wide, —
Nor gun nor scythe to see.
Sure some god his eye enchants:
What he knows nobody wants.
In the wood he travels glad,
Without better fortune had,
Melancholy without bad.
Knowledge this man prizes best
Seems fantastic to the rest:
Pondering shadows, colors, clouds,
Grass-buds and caterpillar-shrouds,
Boughs on which the wild bees settle,
Tints that spot the violet's petal,
Why Nature loves the number five,
And why the star-form she repeats:
Lover of all things alive,
Wonderer at all he meets,
Wonderer chiefly at himself,

Who can tell him what he is?
Or how meet in human elf
Coming and past eternities?

2

And such I knew, a forest seer,
A minstrel of the natural year,
Foreteller of the vernal ides,
Wise harbinger of spheres and tides,
A lover true, who knew by heart
Each joy the mountain dales impart;
It seemed that Nature could not raise
A plant in any secret place,
In quaking bog, on snowy hill,
Beneath the grass that shades the rill,
Under the snow, between the rocks,
In damp fields known to bird and fox.
But he would come in the very hour
It opened in its virgin bower,
As if a sunbeam showed the place,
And tell its long-descended race.
It seemed as if the breezes brought him,
It seemed as if the sparrows taught him;
As if by secret sight he knew
Where, in far fields, the orchis grew.
Many haps fall in the field
Seldom seen by wishful eyes,
But all her shows did Nature yield,
To please and win this pilgrim wise.
He saw the partridge drum in the woods;
He heard the woodcock's evening hymn;
He found the tawny thrushes' broods;
And the shy hawk did wait for him;
What others did at distance hear,

And guessed within the thicket's gloom,
Was shown to this philosopher,
And at his bidding seemed to come.

3

In unploughed Maine he sought the lumberers' gang
Where from a hundred lakes young rivers sprang;
He trode the unplanted forest floor, whereon
The all-seeing sun for ages hath not shone;
Where feeds the moose, and walks the surly bear,
And up the tall mast runs the woodpecker.
He saw beneath dim aisles, in odorous beds,
The slight Linnaea hang its twin-born heads,
And blessed the monument of the man of flowers,
Which breathes his sweet fame through the northern bowers.
He heard, when in the grove, at intervals,
With sudden roar the aged pine-tree falls, —
One crash, the death-hymn of the perfect tree,
Declares the close of its green century.
Low lies the plant to whose creation went
Sweet influence from every element;
Whose living towers the years conspired to build,
Whose giddy top the morning loved to gild.
Through these green tents, by eldest Nature dressed,
He roamed, content alike with man and beast.
Where darkness found him he lay glad at night;
There the red morning touched him with its light.
Three moons his great heart him a hermit made,
So long he roved at will the boundless shade.
The timid it concerns to ask their way,
And fear what foe in caves and swamps can stray,
To make no step until the event is known,
And ills to come as evils past bemoan.
Not so the wise; no coward watch he keeps

To spy what danger on his pathway creeps;
Go where he will, the wise man is at home,
His hearth the earth,—his hall the azure dome;
Where his clear spirit leads him, there's his road
By God's own light illumined and foreshowed.

4

'T was one of the charmèd days
When the genius of God doth flow;
The wind may alter twenty ways,
A tempest cannot blow;
It may blow north, it still is warm;
Or south, it still is clear;
Or east, it smells like a clover-farm;
Or west, no thunder fear.
The musing peasant, lowly great,
Beside the forest water sate;
The rope-like pine-roots crosswise grown
Composed the network of his throne;
The wide lake, edged with sand and grass,
Was burnished to a floor of glass,
Painted with shadows green and proud
Of the tree and of the cloud.
He was the heart of all the scene;
On him the sun looked more serene;
To hill and cloud his face was known,—
It seemed the likeness of their own;
They knew by secret sympathy
The public child of earth and sky.
'You ask,' he said, 'what guide
Me through trackless thickets led,
Through thick-stemmed woodlands rough and wide.
I found the water's bed.
The watercourses were my guide;

I travelled grateful by their side,
Or through their channel dry;
They led me through the thicket damp,
Through brake and fern, the beavers' camp,
Through beds of granite cut my road,
And their resistless friendship showed.
The falling waters led me,
The foodful waters fed me,
And brought me to the lowest land,
Unerring to the ocean sand.
The moss upon the forest bark
Was pole-star when the night was dark;
The purple berries in the wood
Supplied me necessary food;
For Nature ever faithful is
To such as trust her faithfulness.
When the forest shall mislead me,
When the night and morning lie,
When sea and land refuse to feed me,
'T will be time enough to die;
Then will yet my mother yield
A pillow in her greenest field,
Nor the June flowers scorn to cover
The clay of their departed lover.'

WOODNOTES II

As sunbeams stream through liberal space
And nothing jostle or displace,
So waved the pine-tree through my thought
And fanned the dreams it never brought.

'Whether is better, the gift or the donor?
Come to me,'
Quoth the pine-tree,
'I am the giver of honor.
My garden is the cloven rock,
And my manure the snow;
And drifting sand-heaps feed my stock,
In summer's scorching glow.
He is great who can live by me:
The rough and bearded forester
Is better than the lord;
God fills the script and canister,
Sin piles the loaded board.
The lord is the peasant that was,
The peasant the lord that shall be;
The lord is hay, the peasant grass,
One dry, and one the living tree.
Who liveth by the ragged pine
Foundeth a heroic line;
Who liveth in the palace hall
Waneth fast and spendeth all.
He goes to my savage haunts,
With his chariot and his care;

My twilight realm he disenchants,
And finds his prison there.

'What prizes the town and the tower?
Only what the pine-tree yields;
Sinew that subdued the fields;
The wild-eyed boy, who in the woods
Chants his hymn to hills and floods,
Whom the city's poisoning spleen
Made not pale, or fat, or lean;
Whom the rain and the wind purgeth,
Whom the dawn and the day-star urgeth,
In whose cheek the rose-leaf blusheth,
In whose feet the lion rusheth,
Iron arms, and iron mould,
That know not fear, fatigue, or cold.
I give my rafters to his boat,
My billets to his boiler's throat,
And I will swim the ancient sea
To float my child to victory,
And grant to dwellers with the pine
Dominion o'er the palm and vine.
Who leaves the pine-tree, leaves his friend,
Unnerves his strength, invites his end.
Cut a bough from my parent stem,
And dip it in thy porcelain vase;
A little while each russet gem
Will swell and rise with wonted grace;
But when it seeks enlarged supplies,
The orphan of the forest dies.
Whoso walks in solitude
And inhabiteth the wood,
Choosing light, wave, rock and bird,
Before the money-loving herd,
Into that forester shall pass,

From these companions, power and grace.
Clean shall he be, without, within,
From the old adhering sin,
All ill dissolving in the light
Of his triumphant piercing sight:
Not vain, sour, nor frivolous;
Not mad, athirst, nor garrulous;
Grave, chaste, contented, though retired,
And of all other men desired.
On him the light of star and moon
Shall fall with purer radiance down;
All constellations of the sky
Shed their virtue through his eye.
Him Nature giveth for defence
His formidable innocence;
The mounting sap, the shells, the sea,
All spheres, all stones, his helpers be;
He shall meet the speeding year,
Without wailing, without fear;
He shall be happy in his love,
Like to like shall joyful prove;
He shall be happy whilst he wooes,
Muse-born, a daughter of the Muse.
But if with gold she bind her hair,
And deck her breast with diamond,
Take off thine eyes, thy heart forbear,
Though thou lie alone on the ground.

'Heed the old oracles,
Ponder my spells;
Song wakes in my pinnacles
When the wind swells.
Soundeth the prophetic wind,
The shadows shake on the rock behind,
And the countless leaves of the pine are strings

Tuned to the lay the wood-god sings.
Hearken! Hearken!
If thou wouldst know the mystic song
Chanted when the sphere was young.
Aloft, abroad, the paean swells;
O wise man! hear'st thou half it tells?
O wise man! hear'st thou the least part?
'Tis the chronicle of art.
To the open ear it sings
Sweet the genesis of things,
Of tendency through endless ages,
Of star-dust, and star-pilgrimages,
Of rounded worlds, of space and time,
Of the old flood's subsiding slime,
Of chemic matter, force and form,
Of poles and powers, cold, wet, and warm:
The rushing metamorphosis
Dissolving all that fixture is,
Melts things that be to things that seem,
And solid nature to a dream.
O, listen to the undersong,
The ever old, the ever young;
And, far within those cadent pauses,
The chorus of the ancient Causes!
Delights the dreadful Destiny
To fling his voice into the tree,
And shock thy weak ear with a note
Breathed from the everlasting throat.
In music he repeats the pang
Whence the fair flock of Nature sprang.
O mortal! thy ears are stones;
These echoes are laden with tones
Which only the pure can hear;
Thou canst not catch what they recite

Of Fate and Will, of Want and Right,
Of man to come, of human life,
Of Death and Fortune, Growth and Strife.'

Once again the pine-tree sung: —
'Speak not thy speech my boughs among:
Put off thy years, wash in the breeze;
My hours are peaceful centuries.
Talk no more with feeble tongue;
No more the fool of space and time,
Come weave with mine a nobler rhyme.
Only thy Americans
Can read thy line, can meet thy glance,
But the runes that I rehearse
Understands the universe;
The least breath my boughs which tossed
Brings again the Pentecost;
To every soul resounding clear
In a voice of solemn cheer, —
"Am I not thine? Are not these thine?"
And they reply, "Forever mine!"
My branches speak Italian,
English, German, Basque, Castilian,
Mountain speech to Highlanders,
Ocean tongues to islanders,
To Fin and Lap and swart Malay,
To each his bosom-secret say.

'Come learn with me the fatal song
Which knits the world in music strong,
Come lift thine eyes to lofty rhymes,
Of things with things, of times with times,
Primal chimes of sun and shade,
Of sound and echo, man and maid,
The land reflected in the flood,

Body with shadow still pursued.
For Nature beats in perfect tune,
And rounds with rhyme her every rune,
Whether she work in land or sea,
Or hide underground her alchemy.
Thou canst not wave thy staff in air,
Or dip thy paddle in the lake,
But it carves the bow of beauty there,
And the ripples in rhymes the oar forsake.
The wood is wiser far than thou;
The wood and wave each other know
Not unrelated, unaffied,
But to each thought and thing allied,
Is perfect Nature's every part,
Rooted in the mighty Heart,
But thou, poor child! unbound, unrhymed,
Whence camest thou, misplaced, mistimed,
Whence, O thou orphan and defrauded?
Is thy land peeled, thy realm marauded?
Who thee divorced, deceived and left?
Thee of thy faith who hath bereft,
And torn the ensigns from thy brow,
And sunk the immortal eye so low?
Thy cheek too white, thy form too slender,
Thy gait too slow, thy habits tender
For royal man;—they thee confess
An exile from the wilderness,—
The hills where health with health agrees,
And the wise soul expels disease.
Hark! in thy ear I will tell the sign
By which thy hurt thou may'st divine.
When thou shalt climb the mountain cliff,
Or see the wide shore from thy skiff,
To thee the horizon shall express

But emptiness on emptiness;
There lives no man of Nature's worth
In the circle of the earth;
And to thine eye the vast skies fall,
Dire and satirical,
On clucking hens and prating fools,
On thieves, on drudges and on dolls.
And thou shalt say to the Most High,
"Godhead! all this astronomy,
And fate and practice and invention,
Strong art and beautiful pretension,
This radiant pomp of sun and star,
Throes that were, and worlds that are,
Behold! were in vain and in vain;—
It cannot be,—I will look again.
Surely now will the curtain rise,
And earth's fit tenant me surprise;—
But the curtain doth *not* rise,
And Nature has miscarried wholly
Into failure, into folly."

'Alas! thine is the bankruptcy,
Blessed Nature so to see.
Come, lay thee in my soothing shade,
And heal the hurts which sin has made.
I see thee in the crowd alone;
I will be thy companion.
Quit thy friends as the dead in doom,
And build to them a final tomb;
Let the starred shade that nightly falls
Still celebrate their funerals,
And the bell of beetle and of bee
Knell their melodious memory.
Behind thee leave thy merchandise,
Thy churches and thy charities;

And leave thy peacock wit behind;
Enough for thee the primal mind
That flows in streams, that breathes in wind:
Leave all thy pedant lore apart;
God hid the whole world in thy heart.
Love shuns the sage, the child it crowns,
Gives all to them who all renounce.
The rain comes when the wind calls;
The river knows the way to the sea;
Without a pilot it runs and falls,
Blessing all lands with its charity;
The sea tosses and foams to find
Its way up to the cloud and wind;
The shadow sits close to the flying ball;
The date fails not on the palm-tree tall;
And thou,—go burn thy wormy pages,—
Shalt outsee seers, and outwit sages.
Oft didst thou thread the woods in vain
To find what bird had piped the strain:—
Seek not, and the little eremite
Flies gayly forth and sings in sight.

'Hearken once more!
I will tell thee the mundane lore.
Older am I than thy numbers wot,
Change I may, but I pass not.
Hitherto all things fast abide,
And anchored in the tempest ride.
Trenchant time behoves to hurry
All to yean and all to bury:
All the forms are fugitive,
But the substances survive.
Ever fresh the broad creation,
A divine improvisation,
From the heart of God proceeds,

A single will, a million deeds.
Once slept the world an egg of stone,
And pulse, and sound, and light was none;
And God said, "Throb!" and there was motion
And the vast mass became vast ocean.
Onward and on, the eternal Pan,
Who layeth the world's incessant plan,
Halteth never in one shape,
But forever doth escape,
Like wave or flame, into new forms
Of gem, and air, of plants, and worms.
I, that to-day am a pine,
Yesterday was a bundle of grass.
He is free and libertine,
Pouring of his power the wine
To every age, to every race;
Unto every race and age
He emptieth the beverage;
Unto each, and unto all,
Maker and original.
The world is the ring of his spells,
And the play of his miracles.
As he giveth to all to drink,
Thus or thus they are and think.
With one drop sheds form and feature;
With the next a special nature;
The third adds heat's indulgent spark;
The fourth gives light which eats the dark;
Into the fifth himself he flings,
And conscious Law is King of kings.
As the bee through the garden ranges,
From world to world the godhead changes;
As the sheep go feeding in the waste,
From form to form He maketh haste;

This vault which glows immense with light
Is the inn where he lodges for a night.
What recks such Traveller if the bowers
Which bloom and fade like meadow flowers
A bunch of fragrant lilies be,
Or the stars of eternity?
Alike to him the better, the worse,—
The glowing angel, the outcast corse.
Thou metest him by centuries,
And lo! he passes like the breeze;
Thou seek'st in globe and galaxy,
He hides in pure transparency;
Thou askest in fountains and in fires,
He is the essence that inquires.
He is the axis of the star;
He is the sparkle of the spar;
He is the heart of every creature;
He is the meaning of each feature;
And his mind is the sky.
Than all it holds more deep, more high.'

MONADNOC

Thousand minstrels woke within me,
'Our music's in the hills;' —
Gayest pictures rose to win me,
Leopard-colored rills.
'Up! — If thou knew'st who calls
To twilight parks of beech and pine,
High over the river intervals,
Above the ploughman's highest line,
Over the owner's farthest walls!
Up! where the airy citadel
O'erlooks the surging landscape's swell!
Let not unto the stones the Day
Her lily and rose, her sea and land display.
Read the celestial sign!
Lo! the south answers to the north;
Bookworm, break this sloth urbane;
A greater spirit bids thee forth
Than the gray dreams which thee detain.
Mark how the climbing Oreads
Beckon thee to their arcades;
Youth, for a moment free as they,
Teach thy feet to feel the ground,
Ere yet arrives the wintry day
When Time thy feet has bound.
Take the bounty of thy birth,
Taste the lordship of the earth.'

I heard, and I obeyed, —

Assured that he who made the claim,
Well known, but loving not a name,
Was not to be gainsaid.
Ere yet the summoning voice was still,
I turned to Cheshire's haughty hill.
From the fixed cone the cloud-rack flowed
Like ample banner flung abroad
To all the dwellers in the plains
Round about, a hundred miles,
With salutation to the sea and to the bordering isles.
In his own loom's garment dressed,
By his proper bounty blessed,
Fast abides this constant giver,
Pouring many a cheerful river;
To far eyes, an aerial isle
Unploughed, which finer spirits pile,
Which morn and crimson evening paint
For bard, for lover and for saint;
An eyemark and the country's core,
Inspirer, prophet evermore;
Pillar which God aloft had set
So that men might it not forget;
It should be their life's ornament,
And mix itself with each event;
Gauge and calendar and dial,
Weatherglass and chemic phial,
Garden of berries, perch of birds,
Pasture of pool-haunting herds,
Graced by each change of sum untold,
Earth-baking heat, stone-cleaving cold.

The Titan heeds his sky-affairs,
Rich rents and wide alliance shares;
Mysteries of color daily laid
By morn and eve in light and shade;

And sweet varieties of chance,
And the mystic seasons' dance;
And thief-like step of liberal hours
Thawing snow-drift into flowers.
O, wondrous craft of plant and stone
By eldest science wrought and shown!

'Happy,' I said, 'whose home is here!
Fair fortunes to the mountaineer!
Boon Nature to his poorest shed
Has royal pleasure-grounds outspread.'
Intent, I searched the region round,
And in low hut the dweller found:
Woe is me for my hope's downfall!
Is yonder squalid peasant all
That this proud nursery could breed
For God's vicegerency and stead?
Time out of mind, this forge of ores;
Quarry of spars in mountain pores;
Old cradle, hunting-ground and bier
Of wolf and otter, bear and deer;
Well-built abode of many a race;
Tower of observance searching space;
Factory of river and of rain;
Link in the Alps' globe-girding chain;
By million changes skilled to tell
What in the Eternal standeth well,
And what obedient Nature can; —
Is this colossal talisman
Kindly to plant and blood and kind,
But speechless to the master's mind?
I thought to find the patriots
In whom the stock of freedom roots;
To myself I oft recount
Tales of many a famous mount, —

Wales, Scotland, Uri, Hungary's dells:
Bards, Roys, Scanderbegs and Tells;
And think how Nature in these towers
Uplifted shall condense her powers,
And lifting man to the blue deep
Where stars their perfect courses keep,
Like wise preceptor, lure his eye
To sound the science of the sky,
And carry learning to its height
Of untried power and sane delight:
The Indian cheer, the frosty skies,
Rear purer wits, inventive eyes,—
Eyes that frame cities where none be,
And hands that stablish what these see:
And by the moral of his place
Hint summits of heroic grace;
Man in these crags a fastness find
To fight pollution of the mind;
In the wide thaw and ooze of wrong,
Adhere like this foundation strong,
The insanity of towns to stem
With simpleness for stratagem.
But if the brave old mould is broke,
And end in churls the mountain folk
In tavern cheer and tavern joke,
Sink, O mountain, in the swamp!
Hide in thy skies, O sovereign lamp!
Perish like leaves, the highland breed
No sire survive, no son succeed!

Soft! let not the offended muse
Toil's hard hap with scorn accuse.
Many hamlets sought I then,
Many farms of mountain men.
Rallying round a parish steeple

Nestle warm the highland people,
Coarse and boisterous, yet mild,
Strong as giant, slow as child.
Sweat and season are their arts,
Their talismans are ploughs and carts;
And well the youngest can command
Honey from the frozen land;
With cloverheads the swamp adorn,
Change the running sand to corn;
For wolf and fox, bring lowing herds,
And for cold mosses, cream and curds:
Weave wood to canisters and mats;
Drain sweet maple juice in vats.
No bird is safe that cuts the air
From their rifle or their snare;
No fish, in river or in lake,
But their long hands it thence will take;
Whilst the country's flinty face,
Like wax, their fashioning skill betrays,
To fill the hollows, sink the hills,
Bridge gulfs, drain swamps, build dams and mills,
And fit the bleak and howling waste
For homes of virtue, sense and taste.
The World-soul knows his own affair,
Forelooking, when he would prepare
For the next ages, men of mould
Well embodied, well ensouled,
He cools the present's fiery glow,
Sets the life-pulse strong but slow:
Bitter winds and fasts austere
His quarantines and grottoes, where
He slowly cures decrepit flesh,
And brings it infantile and fresh.
Toil and tempest are the toys

And games to breathe his stalwart boys:
They bide their time, and well can prove,
If need were, their line from Jove;
Of the same stuff, and so allayed,
As that whereof the sun is made,
And of the fibre, quick and strong,
Whose throbs are love, whose thrills are song.

Now in sordid weeds they sleep,
In dulness now their secret keep;
Yet, will you learn our ancient speech,
These the masters who can teach.
Fourscore or a hundred words
All their vocal muse affords;
But they turn them in a fashion
Past clerks' or statesmen's art or passion.
I can spare the college bell,
And the learned lecture, well;
Spare the clergy and libraries,
Institutes and dictionaries,
For that hardy English root
Thrives here, unvalued, underfoot.
Rude poets of the tavern hearth,
Squandering your unquoted mirth,
Which keeps the ground and never soars,
While Jake retorts and Reuben roars;
Scoff of yeoman strong and stark,
Goes like bullet to its mark;
While the solid curse and jeer
Never balk the waiting ear.

On the summit as I stood,
O'er the floor of plain and flood
Seemed to me, the towering hill
Was not altogether still,

But a quiet sense conveyed:
If I err not, thus it said:—

'Many feet in summer seek,
Oft, my far-appearing peak;
In the dreaded winter time,
None save dappling shadows climb,
Under clouds, my lonely head,
Old as the sun, old almost as the shade;
And comest thou
To see strange forests and new snow,
And tread uplifted land?
And leavest thou thy lowland race,
Here amid clouds to stand?
And wouldst be my companion
Where I gaze, and still shall gaze,
Through tempering nights and flashing days,
When forests fall, and man is gone,
Over tribes and over times,
At the burning Lyre,
Nearing me,
With its stars of northern fire,
In many a thousand years?

'Gentle pilgrim, if thou know
The gamut old of Pan,
And how the hills began,
The frank blessings of the hill
Fall on thee, as fall they will.

'Let him heed who can and will;
Enchantment fixed me here
To stand the hurts of time, until
In mightier chant I disappear.
If thou trowest
How the chemic eddies play,

Pole to pole, and what they say;
And that these gray crags
Not on crags are hung,
But beads are of a rosary
On prayer and music strung;
And, credulous, through the granite seeming,
Seest the smile of Reason beaming;—
Can thy style-discerning eye
The hidden-working Builder spy,
Who builds, yet makes no chips, no din,
With hammer soft as snowflake's flight;—
Knowest thou this?
O pilgrim, wandering not amiss!
Already my rocks lie light,
And soon my cone will spin.

'For the world was built in order,
And the atoms march in tune;
Rhyme the pipe, and Time the warder,
The sun obeys them and the moon.
Orb and atom forth they prance,
When they hear from far the rune;
None so backward in the troop,
When the music and the dance
Reach his place and circumstance,
But knows the sun-creating sound,
And, though a pyramid, will bound.

'Monadnoc is a mountain strong,
Tall and good my kind among;
But well I know, no mountain can,
Zion or Meru, measure with man.
For it is on zodiacs writ,
Adamant is soft to wit:
And when the greater comes again

With my secret in his brain,
I shall pass, as glides my shadow
Daily over hill and meadow.

'Through all time, in light, in gloom
Well I hear the approaching feet
On the flinty pathway beat
Of him that cometh, and shall come;
Of him who shall as lightly bear
My daily load of woods and streams,
As doth this round sky-cleaving boat
Which never strains its rocky beams;
Whose timbers, as they silent float,
Alps and Caucasus uprear,
And the long Alleghanies here,
And all town-sprinkled lands that be,
Sailing through stars with all their history.

'Every morn I lift my head,
See New England underspread,
South from Saint Lawrence to the Sound,
From Katskill east to the sea-bound.
Anchored fast for many an age,
I await the bard and sage,
Who, in large thoughts, like fair pearl-seed,
Shall string Monadnoc like a bead.
Comes that cheerful troubadour,
This mound shall throb his face before,
As when, with inward fires and pain,
It rose a bubble from the plain.
When he cometh, I shall shed,
From this wellspring in my head,
Fountain-drop of spicier worth
Than all vintage of the earth.
There's fruit upon my barren soil

Costlier far than wine or oil.
There's a berry blue and gold, —
Autumn-ripe, its juices hold
Sparta's stoutness, Bethlehem's heart,
Asia's rancor, Athens' art,
Slowsure Britain's secular might,
And the German's inward sight.
I will give my son to eat
Best of Pan's immortal meat,
Bread to eat, and juice to drain;
So the coinage of his brain
Shall not be forms of stars, but stars,
Nor pictures pale, but Jove and Mars,
He comes, but not of that race bred
Who daily climb my specular head.
Oft as morning wreathes my scarf,
Fled the last plumule of the Dark,
Pants up hither the spruce clerk
From South Cove and City Wharf.
I take him up my rugged sides,
Half-repentant, scant of breath, —
Bead-eyes my granite chaos show,
And my midsummer snow:
Open the daunting map beneath, —
All his county, sea and land,
Dwarfed to measure of his hand;
His day's ride is a furlong space,
His city-tops a glimmering haze.
I plant his eyes on the sky-hoop bounding;
"See there the grim gray rounding
Of the bullet of the earth
Whereon ye sail,
Tumbling steep
In the uncontinented deep."

He looks on that, and he turns pale.
'T is even so, this treacherous kite,
Farm-furrowed, town-incrusted sphere,
Thoughtless of its anxious freight,
Plunges eyeless on forever;
And he, poor parasite,
Cooped in a ship he cannot steer,—
Who is the captain he knows not,
Port or pilot trows not,—
Risk or ruin he must share.
I scowl on him with my cloud,
With my north wind chill his blood;
I lame him, clattering down the rocks;
And to live he is in fear.
Then, at last, I let him down
Once more into his dapper town,
To chatter, frightened, to his clan
And forget me if he can.'

As in the old poetic fame
The gods are blind and lame,
And the simular despite
Betrays the more abounding might,
So call not waste that barren cone
Above the floral zone,
Where forests starve:
It is pure use;—
What sheaves like those which here we glean and bind
Of a celestial Ceres and the Muse?

Ages are thy days,
Thou grand affirmer of the present tense,
And type of permanence!
Firm ensign of the fatal Being,
Amid these coward shapes of joy and grief,

That will not bide the seeing!

Hither we bring
Our insect miseries to thy rocks;
And the whole flight, with folded wing,
Vanish, and end their murmuring, —
Vanish beside these dedicated blocks,
Which who can tell what mason laid?
Spoils of a front none need restore,
Replacing frieze and architrave; —
Where flowers each stone rosette and metope brave;
Still is the haughty pile erect
Of the old building Intellect.

Complement of human kind,
Holding us at vantage still,
Our sumptuous indigence,
O barren mound, thy plenties fill!
We fool and prate;
Thou art silent and sedate.
To myriad kinds and times one sense
The constant mountain doth dispense;
Shedding on all its snows and leaves,
One joy it joys, one grief it grieves.
Thou seest, O watchman tall,
Our towns and races grow and fall,
And imagest the stable good
For which we all our lifetime grope,
In shifting form the formless mind,
And though the substance us elude,
We in thee the shadow find.
Thou, in our astronomy
An opaker star,
Seen haply from afar,
Above the horizon's hoop,

A moment, by the railway troop,
As o'er some bolder height they speed, —
By circumspect ambition,
By errant gain,
By feasters and the frivolous, —
Recallest us,
And makest sane.
Mute orator! well skilled to plead,
And send conviction without phrase,
Thou dost succor and remede
The shortness of our days,
And promise, on thy Founder's truth,
Long morrow to this mortal youth.

FABLE

The mountain and the squirrel
Had a quarrel,
And the former called the latter 'Little Prig;
Bun replied,
'You are doubtless very big;
But all sorts of things and weather
Must be taken in together,
To make up a year
And a sphere.
And I think it no disgrace
To occupy my place.
If I'm not so large as you,
You are not so small as I,
And not half so spry.
I'll not deny you make
A very pretty squirrel track;
Talents differ; all is well and wisely put;
If I cannot carry forests on my back,
Neither can you crack a nut.'

ODE

INSCRIBED TO W.H. CHANNING

Though loath to grieve
The evil time's sole patriot,
I cannot leave
My honied thought
For the priest's cant,
Or statesman's rant.

If I refuse
My study for their politique,
Which at the best is trick,
The angry Muse
Puts confusion in my brain.

But who is he that prates
Of the culture of mankind,
Of better arts and life?
Go, blindworm, go,
Behold the famous States
Harrying Mexico
With rifle and with knife!

Or who, with accent bolder,
Dare praise the freedom-loving mountaineer?
I found by thee, O rushing Contoocook!
And in thy valleys, Agiochook!
The jackals of the negro-holder.

The God who made New Hampshire

Taunted the lofty land
With little men;—
Small bat and wren
House in the oak:—
If earth-fire cleave
The upheaved land, and bury the folk,
The southern crocodile would grieve.
Virtue palters; Right is hence;
Freedom praised, but hid;
Funeral eloquence
Rattles the coffin-lid.

What boots thy zeal,
O glowing friend,
That would indignant rend
The northland from the south?
Wherefore? to what good end?
Boston Bay and Bunker Hill
Would serve things still;—
Things are of the snake.

The horseman serves the horse,
The neatherd serves the neat,
The merchant serves the purse,
The eater serves his meat;
'T is the day of the chattel,
Web to weave, and corn to grind;
Things are in the saddle,
And ride mankind.

There are two laws discrete,
Not reconciled,—
Law for man, and law for thing;
The last builds town and fleet,
But it runs wild,
And doth the man unking.

'T is fit the forest fall,
The steep be graded,
The mountain tunnelled,
The sand shaded,
The orchard planted,
The glebe tilled,
The prairie granted,
The steamer built.

Let man serve law for man;
Live for friendship, live for love,
For truth's and harmony's behoof;
The state may follow how it can,
As Olympus follows Jove.

Yet do not I implore
The wrinkled shopman to my sounding woods,
Nor bid the unwilling senator
Ask votes of thrushes in the solitudes.
Every one to his chosen work; —
Foolish hands may mix and mar;
Wise and sure the issues are.
Round they roll till dark is light,
Sex to sex, and even to odd; —
The over-god
Who marries Right to Might,
Who peoples, unpeoples, —
He who exterminates
Races by stronger races,
Black by white faces, —
Knows to bring honey
Out of the lion;
Grafts gentlest scion
On pirate and Turk.

The Cossack eats Poland,

Like stolen fruit;
Her last noble is ruined,
Her last poet mute:
Straight, into double band
The victors divide;
Half for freedom strike and stand;—
The astonished Muse finds thousands at her side.

ASTRAEA

Each the herald is who wrote
His rank, and quartered his own coat.
There is no king nor sovereign state
That can fix a hero's rate;
Each to all is venerable,
Cap-a-pie invulnerable,
Until he write, where all eyes rest,
Slave or master on his breast.
I saw men go up and down,
In the country and the town,
With this tablet on their neck,
'Judgment and a judge we seek.'
Not to monarchs they repair,
Nor to learned jurist's chair;
But they hurry to their peers,
To their kinsfolk and their dears;
Louder than with speech they pray,—
'What am I? companion, say.'
And the friend not hesitates
To assign just place and mates;
Answers not in word or letter,
Yet is understood the better;
Each to each a looking-glass,
Reflects his figure that doth pass.
Every wayfarer he meets
What himself declared repeats,
What himself confessed records,
Sentences him in his words;

The form is his own corporal form,
And his thought the penal worm.
Yet shine forever virgin minds,
Loved by stars and purest winds,
Which, o'er passion throned sedate,
Have not hazarded their state;
Disconcert the searching spy,
Rendering to a curious eye
The durance of a granite ledge.
To those who gaze from the sea's edge
It is there for benefit;
It is there for purging light;
There for purifying storms;
And its depths reflect all forms;
It cannot parley with the mean, —
Pure by impure is not seen.
For there's no sequestered grot,
Lone mountain tarn, or isle forgot,
But Justice, journeying in the sphere,
Daily stoops to harbor there.

ÉTIENNE DE LA BOÉCE

I serve you not, if you I follow,
Shadowlike, o'er hill and hollow;
And bend my fancy to your leading,
All too nimble for my treading.
When the pilgrimage is done,
And we've the landscape overrun,
I am bitter, vacant, thwarted,
And your heart is unsupported.
Vainly valiant, you have missed
The manhood that should yours resist, —
Its complement; but if I could,
In severe or cordial mood,

Lead you rightly to my altar,
Where the wisest Muses falter,
And worship that world-warming spark
Which dazzles me in midnight dark,
Equalizing small and large,
While the soul it doth surcharge,
Till the poor is wealthy grown,
And the hermit never alone, —
The traveller and the road seem one
With the errand to be done, —
That were a man's and lover's part,
That were Freedom's whitest chart.

COMPENSATION

Why should I keep holiday
When other men have none?
Why but because, when these are gay,
I sit and mourn alone?

And why, when mirth unseals all tongues,
Should mine alone be dumb?
Ah! late I spoke to silent throngs,
And now their hour is come.

FORBEARANCE

Hast thou named all the birds without a gun?
Loved the wood-rose, and left it on its stalk?
At rich men's tables eaten bread and pulse?
Unarmed, faced danger with a heart of trust?
And loved so well a high behavior,
In man or maid, that thou from speech refrained,
Nobility more nobly to repay?
O, be my friend, and teach me to be thine!

THE PARK

The prosperous and beautiful
To me seem not to wear
The yoke of conscience masterful,
Which galls me everywhere.

I cannot shake off the god;
On my neck he makes his seat;
I look at my face in the glass,—
My eyes his eyeballs meet.

Enchanters! Enchantresses!
Your gold makes you seem wise;
The morning mist within your grounds
More proudly rolls, more softly lies.

Yet spake yon purple mountain,
Yet said yon ancient wood,
That Night or Day, that Love or Crime,
Leads all souls to the Good.

FORERUNNERS

Long I followed happy guides,
I could never reach their sides;
Their step is forth, and, ere the day
Breaks up their leaguer, and away.
Keen my sense, my heart was young,
Right good-will my sinews strung,
But no speed of mine avails
To hunt upon their shining trails.
On and away, their hasting feet
Make the morning proud and sweet;
Flowers they strew,—I catch the scent;
Or tone of silver instrument
Leaves on the wind melodious trace;
Yet I could never see their face.
On eastern hills I see their smokes,
Mixed with mist by distant lochs.
I met many travellers
Who the road had surely kept;
They saw not my fine revellers,—
These had crossed them while they slept.
Some had heard their fair report,
In the country or the court.
Fleetest couriers alive
Never yet could once arrive,
As they went or they returned,
At the house where these sojourned.
Sometimes their strong speed they slacken,

Though they are not overtaken;
In sleep their jubilant troop is near,—
I tuneful voices overhear;
It may be in wood or waste,—
At unawares 't is come and past.
Their near camp my spirit knows
By signs gracious as rainbows.
I thenceforward and long after
Listen for their harp-like laughter,
And carry in my heart, for days,
Peace that hallows rudest ways.

SURSUM CORDA

Seek not the spirit, if it hide
Inexorable to thy zeal:
Trembler, do not whine and chide:
Art thou not also real?
Stoop not then to poor excuse;
Turn on the accuser roundly; say,
'Here am I, here will I abide
Forever to myself soothfast;
Go thou, sweet Heaven, or at thy pleasure stay!'
Already Heaven with thee its lot has cast,
For only it can absolutely deal.

ODE TO BEAUTY

Who gave thee, O Beauty,
The keys of this breast, —
Too credulous lover
Of blest and unblest?
Say, when in lapsed ages
Thee knew I of old?
Or what was the service
For which I was sold?
When first my eyes saw thee,
I found me thy thrall,
By magical drawings,
Sweet tyrant of all!
I drank at thy fountain
False waters of thirst;
Thou intimate stranger,
Thou latest and first!
Thy dangerous glances
Make women of men;
New-born, we are melting
Into nature again.

Lavish, lavish promiser,
Nigh persuading gods to err!
Guest of million painted forms,
Which in turn thy glory warms!
The frailest leaf, the mossy bark,
The acorn's cup, the raindrop's arc,
The swinging spider's silver line,

The ruby of the drop of wine,
The shining pebble of the pond,
Thou inscribest with a bond,
In thy momentary play,
Would bankrupt nature to repay.

Ah, what avails it
To hide or to shun
Whom the Infinite One
Hath granted his throne?
The heaven high over
Is the deep's lover;
The sun and sea,
Informed by thee,
Before me run
And draw me on,
Yet fly me still,
As Fate refuses
To me the heart Fate for me chooses.
Is it that my opulent soul
Was mingled from the generous whole;
Sea-valleys and the deep of skies
Furnished several supplies;
And the sands whereof I'm made
Draw me to them, self-betrayed?

I turn the proud portfolio
Which holds the grand designs
Of Salvator, of Guercino,
And Piranesi's lines.
I hear the lofty paeans
Of the masters of the shell,
Who heard the starry music
And recount the numbers well;
Olympian bards who sung

Divine Ideas below,
Which always find us young
And always keep us so.
Oft, in streets or humblest places,
I detect far-wandered graces,
Which, from Eden wide astray,
In lowly homes have lost their way.

Thee gliding through the sea of form,
Like the lightning through the storm,
Somewhat not to be possessed,
Somewhat not to be caressed,
No feet so fleet could ever find,
No perfect form could ever bind.
Thou eternal fugitive,
Hovering over all that live,
Quick and skilful to inspire
Sweet, extravagant desire,
Starry space and lily-bell
Filling with thy roseate smell,
Wilt not give the lips to taste
Of the nectar which thou hast.

All that's good and great with thee
Works in close conspiracy;
Thou hast bribed the dark and lonely
To report thy features only,
And the cold and purple morning
Itself with thoughts of thee adorning;
The leafy dell, the city mart,
Equal trophies of thine art;
E'en the flowing azure air
Thou hast touched for my despair;
And, if I languish into dreams,
Again I meet the ardent beams.

Queen of things! I dare not die
In Being's deeps past ear and eye;
Lest there I find the same deceiver
And be the sport of Fate forever.
Dread Power, but dear! if God thou be,
Unmake me quite, or give thyself to me!

GIVE ALL TO LOVE

Give all to love;
Obey thy heart;
Friends, kindred, days,
Estate, good-fame,
Plans, credit and the Muse,—
Nothing refuse.

'T is a brave master;
Let it have scope:
Follow it utterly,
Hope beyond hope:
High and more high
It dives into noon,
With wing unspent,
Untold intent;
But it is a god,
Knows its own path
And the outlets of the sky.

It was never for the mean;
It requireth courage stout.
Souls above doubt,
Valor unbending,
It will reward,—
They shall return
More than they were,
And ever ascending.

Leave all for love;
Yet, hear me, yet,

One word more thy heart behoved,
One pulse more of firm endeavor,—
Keep thee to-day,
To-morrow, forever,
Free as an Arab
Of thy beloved.

Cling with life to the maid;
But when the surprise,
First vague shadow of surmise
Flits across her bosom young,
Of a joy apart from thee,
Free be she, fancy-free;
Nor thou detain her vesture's hem,
Nor the palest rose she flung
From her summer diadem.

Though thou loved her as thyself,
As a self of purer clay,
Though her parting dims the day,
Stealing grace from all alive;
Heartily know,
When half-gods go.
The gods arrive.

TO ELLEN AT THE SOUTH

The green grass is bowing,
The morning wind is in it;
'T is a tune worth thy knowing,
Though it change every minute.

'T is a tune of the Spring;
Every year plays it over
To the robin on the wing,
And to the pausing lover.

O'er ten thousand, thousand acres,
Goes light the nimble zephyr;
The Flowers—tiny sect of Shakers—
Worship him ever.

Hark to the winning sound!
They summon thee, dearest,—
Saying, 'We have dressed for thee the ground,
Nor yet thou appearest.

'O hasten;' 't is our time,
Ere yet the red Summer
Scorch our delicate prime,
Loved of bee,—the tawny hummer.

'O pride of thy race!
Sad, in sooth, it were to ours,
If our brief tribe miss thy face,
We poor New England flowers.

'Fairest, choose the fairest members
Of our lithe society;

June's glories and September's
Show our love and piety.

'Thou shalt command us all,—
April's cowslip, summer's clover,
To the gentian in the fall,
Blue-eyed pet of blue-eyed lover.

'O come, then, quickly come!
We are budding, we are blowing;
And the wind that we perfume
Sings a tune that's worth the knowing.'

TO ELLEN

And Ellen, when the graybeard years
Have brought us to life's evening hour,
And all the crowded Past appears
A tiny scene of sun and shower,

Then, if I read the page aright
Where Hope, the soothsayer, reads our lot,
Thyself shalt own the page was bright,
Well that we loved, woe had we not,

When Mirth is dumb and Flattery's fled,
And mute thy music's dearest tone,
When all but Love itself is dead
And all but deathless Reason gone.

TO EVA

O fair and stately maid, whose eyes
Were kindled in the upper skies
At the same torch that lighted mine;
For so I must interpret still
Thy sweet dominion o'er my will,
A sympathy divine.

Ah! let me blameless gaze upon
Features that seem at heart my own;
Nor fear those watchful sentinels,
Who charm the more their glance forbids,
Chaste-glowing, underneath their lids,
With fire that draws while it repels.

LINES

WRITTEN BY ELLEN LOUISA TUCKER SHORTLY
BEFORE
HER MARRIAGE TO MR. EMERSON

Love scatters oil
On Life's dark sea,
Sweetens its toil—
Our helmsman he.

Around him hover
Odorous clouds;
Under this cover
His arrows he shrouds.

The cloud was around me,
I knew not why
Such sweetness crowned me.
While Time shot by.

No pain was within,
But calm delight,
Like a world without sin,
Or a day without night.

The shafts of the god
Were tipped with down,
For they drew no blood,
And they knit no frown.

I knew of them not
Until Cupid laughed loud,

And saying "You're caught!"
Flew off in the cloud.

O then I awoke,
And I lived but to sigh,
Till a clear voice spoke, —
And my tears are dry.

THE VIOLET

BY ELLEN LOUISA TUCKER

Why lingerest thou, pale violet, to see the dying year;
Are Autumn's blasts fit music for thee, fragile one, to hear;
Will thy clear blue eye, upward bent, still keep its chastened glow,
Still tearless lift its slender form above the wintry snow?

Why wilt thou live when none around reflects thy pensive ray?
Thou bloomest here a lonely thing in the clear autumn day.
The tall green trees, that shelter thee, their last gay dress put on;
There will be nought to shelter thee when their sweet leaves are gone.

O Violet, like thee, how blest could I lie down and die,
When summer light is fading, and autumn breezes sigh;
When Winter reigned I'd close my eye, but wake with bursting Spring,
And live with living nature, a pure rejoicing thing.

I had a sister once who seemed just like a violet;
Her morning sun shone bright and calmly purely set;
When the violets were in their shrouds, and Summer in its pride,
She laid her hopes at rest, and in the year's rich beauty died.

THE AMULET

Your picture smiles as first it smiled;
The ring you gave is still the same;
Your letter tells, O changing child!
No tidings *since* it came.

Give me an amulet
That keeps intelligence with you,—
Red when you love, and rosier red,
And when you love not, pale and blue.

Alas! that neither bonds nor vows
Can certify possession;
Torments me still the fear that love
Died in its last expression.

THINE EYES STILL SHINED

Thine eyes still shined for me, though far
I lonely roved the land or sea:
As I behold yon evening star,
Which yet beholds not me.

This morn I climbed the misty hill
And roamed the pastures through;
How danced thy form before my path
Amidst the deep-eyed dew!

When the redbird spread his sable wing,
And showed his side of flame;
When the rosebud ripened to the rose,
In both I read thy name.

EROS

The sense of the world is short, —
Long and various the report, —
To love and be beloved;
Men and gods have not outlearned it;
And, how oft soe'er they've turned it,
Not to be improved.

HERMIONE

On a mound an Arab lay,
And sung his sweet regrets
And told his amulets:
The summer bird
His sorrow heard,
And, when he heaved a sigh profound,
The sympathetic swallow swept the ground.

'If it be, as they said, she was not fair,
Beauty's not beautiful to me,
But sceptred genius, aye inorbed,
Culminating in her sphere.
This Hermione absorbed
The lustre of the land and ocean,
Hills and islands, cloud and tree,
In her form and motion.

'I ask no bauble miniature,
Nor ringlets dead
Shorn from her comely head,
Now that morning not disdains
Mountains and the misty plains
Her colossal portraiture;
They her heralds be,
Steeped in her quality,
And singers of her fame
Who is their Muse and dame.

'Higher, dear swallows! mind not what I say.
Ah! heedless how the weak are strong,

Say, was it just,
In thee to frame, in me to trust,
Thou to the Syrian couldst belong?

'I am of a lineage
That each for each doth fast engage;
In old Bassora's schools, I seemed
Hermit vowed to books and gloom,—
Ill-bestead for gay bridegroom.
I was by thy touch redeemed;
When thy meteor glances came,
We talked at large of worldly fate,
And drew truly every trait.

'Once I dwelt apart,
Now I live with all;
As shepherd's lamp on far hill-side
Seems, by the traveller espied,
A door into the mountain heart,
So didst thou quarry and unlock
Highways for me through the rock.

'Now, deceived, thou wanderest
In strange lands unblest;
And my kindred come to soothe me.
Southwind is my next of blood;
He is come through fragrant wood,
Drugged with spice from climates warm,
And in every twinkling glade,
And twilight nook,
Unveils thy form.
Out of the forest way
Forth paced it yesterday;
And when I sat by the watercourse,
Watching the daylight fade,
It throbbed up from the brook.

'River and rose and crag and bird,
Frost and sun and eldest night,
To me their aid preferred,
To me their comfort plight;—
"Courage! we are thine allies,
And with this hint be wise,—
The chains of kind
The distant bind;
Deed thou doest she must do,
Above her will, be true;
And, in her strict resort
To winds and waterfalls
And autumn's sunlit festivals,
To music, and to music's thought,
Inextricably bound,
She shall find thee, and be found.
Follow not her flying feet;
Come to us herself to meet."'

INITIAL, DAEMONIC AND CELESTIAL LOVE

I. THE INITIAL LOVE

Venus, when her son was lost,
Cried him up and down the coast,
In hamlets, palaces and parks,
And told the truant by his marks, —
Golden curls, and quiver and bow.
This befell how long ago!
Time and tide are strangely changed,
Men and manners much deranged:
None will now find Cupid latent
By this foolish antique patent.
He came late along the waste,
Shod like a traveller for haste;
With malice dared me to proclaim him,
That the maids and boys might name him.

Boy no more, he wears all coats,
Frocks and blouses, capes, capotes;
He bears no bow, or quiver, or wand,
Nor chaplet on his head or hand.
Leave his weeds and heed his eyes, —
All the rest he can disguise.
In the pit of his eye's a spark
Would bring back day if it were dark;
And, if I tell you all my thought,
Though I comprehend it not,
In those unfathomable orbs
Every function he absorbs;

Doth eat, and drink, and fish, and shoot,
And write, and reason, and compute,
And ride, and run, and have, and hold,
And whine, and flatter, and regret,
And kiss, and couple, and beget,
By those roving eyeballs bold.

Undaunted are their courages,
Right Cossacks in their forages;
Fleeter they than any creature,—
They are his steeds, and not his feature;
Inquisitive, and fierce, and fasting,
Restless, predatory, hasting;
And they pounce on other eyes
As lions on their prey;
And round their circles is writ,
Plainer than the day,
Underneath, within, above,—
Love—love—love—love.
He lives in his eyes;
There doth digest, and work, and spin,
And buy, and sell, and lose, and win;
He rolls them with delighted motion,
Joy-tides swell their mimic ocean.
Yet holds he them with tautest rein,
That they may seize and entertain
The glance that to their glance opposes,
Like fiery honey sucked from roses.
He palmistry can understand,
Imbibing virtue by his hand
As if it were a living root;
The pulse of hands will make him mute;
With all his force he gathers balms
Into those wise, thrilling palms.

Cupid is a casuist,

A mystic and a cabalist, —
Can your lurking thought surprise,
And interpret your device.
He is versed in occult science,
In magic and in clairvoyance,
Oft he keeps his fine ear strained,
And Reason on her tiptoe pained
For aëry intelligence,
And for strange coincidence.
But it touches his quick heart
When Fate by omens takes his part,
And chance-dropped hints from Nature's sphere
Deeply soothe his anxious ear.

Heralds high before him run;
He has ushers many a one;
He spreads his welcome where he goes,
And touches all things with his rose.
All things wait for and divine him, —
How shall I dare to malign him,
Or accuse the god of sport?
I must end my true report,
Painting him from head to foot,
In as far as I took note,
Trusting well the matchless power
Of this young-eyed emperor
Will clear his fame from every cloud
With the bards and with the crowd.

He is wilful, mutable,
Shy, untamed, inscrutable,
Swifter-fashioned than the fairies.
Substance mixed of pure contraries;
His vice some elder virtue's token,
And his good is evil-spoken.

Failing sometimes of his own,
He is headstrong and alone;
He affects the wood and wild,
Like a flower-hunting child;
Buries himself in summer waves,
In trees, with beasts, in mines and caves,
Loves nature like a hornèd cow,
Bird, or deer, or caribou.

Shun him, nymphs, on the fleet horses!
He has a total world of wit;
O how wise are his discourses!
But he is the arch-hypocrite,
And, through all science and all art,
Seeks alone his counterpart.
He is a Pundit of the East,
He is an augur and a priest,
And his soul will melt in prayer,
But word and wisdom is a snare;
Corrupted by the present toy
He follows joy, and only joy.
There is no mask but he will wear;
He invented oaths to swear;
He paints, he carves, he chants, he prays,
And holds all stars in his embrace.
He takes a sovran privilege
Not allowed to any liege;
For Cupid goes behind all law,
And right into himself does draw;
For he is sovereignly allied, —
Heaven's oldest blood flows in his side, —
And interchangeably at one
With every king on every throne,
That no god dare say him nay,
Or see the fault, or seen betray;

He has the Muses by the heart,
And the stern Parcae on his part.

His many signs cannot be told;
He has not one mode, but manifold,
Many fashions and addresses,
Piques, reproaches, hurts, caresses.
He will preach like a friar,
And jump like Harlequin;
He will read like a crier,
And fight like a Paladin.
Boundless is his memory;
Plans immense his term prolong;
He is not of counted age,
Meaning always to be young.
And his wish is intimacy,
Intimater intimacy,
And a stricter privacy;
The impossible shall yet be done,
And, being two, shall still be one.
As the wave breaks to foam on shelves,
Then runs into a wave again,
So lovers melt their sundered selves,
Yet melted would be twain.

II
THE DAEMONIC LOVE

Man was made of social earth,
Child and brother from his birth,
Tethered by a liquid cord
Of blood through veins of kindred poured.
Next his heart the fireside band
Of mother, father, sister, stand;
Names from awful childhood heard
Throbs of a wild religion stirred;—
Virtue, to love, to hate them, vice;
Till dangerous Beauty came, at last,
Till Beauty came to snap all ties;
The maid, abolishing the past,
With lotus wine obliterates
Dear memory's stone-incarved traits,
And, by herself, supplants alone
Friends year by year more inly known.
When her calm eyes opened bright,
All else grew foreign in their light.
It was ever the self-same tale,
The first experience will not fail;
Only two in the garden walked,
And with snake and seraph talked.

Close, close to men,
Like undulating layer of air,
Right above their heads,
The potent plain of Daemons spreads.

Stands to each human soul its own,
For watch and ward and furtherance,
In the snares of Nature's dance;
And the lustre and the grace
To fascinate each youthful heart,
Beaming from its counterpart,
Translucent through the mortal covers,
Is the Daemon's form and face.
To and fro the Genius hies,—
A gleam which plays and hovers
Over the maiden's head,
And dips sometimes as low as to her eyes.
Unknown, albeit lying near,
To men, the path to the Daemon sphere;
And they that swiftly come and go
Leave no track on the heavenly snow.
Sometimes the airy synod bends,
And the mighty choir descends,
And the brains of men thenceforth,
In crowded and in still resorts,
Teem with unwonted thoughts:
As, when a shower of meteors
Cross the orbit of the earth,
And, lit by fringent air,
Blaze near and far,
Mortals deem the planets bright
Have slipped their sacred bars,
And the lone seaman all the night
Sails, astonished, amid stars.

Beauty of a richer vein,
Graces of a subtler strain,
Unto men these moonmen lend,

And our shrinking sky extend.
So is man's narrow path
By strength and terror skirted;
Also (from the song the wrath
Of the Genii be averted!
The Muse the truth uncolored speaking)
The Daemons are self-seeking:
Their fierce and limitary will
Draws men to their likeness still.
The erring painter made Love blind, —
Highest Love who shines on all;
Him, radiant, sharpest-sighted god,
None can bewilder;
Whose eyes pierce
The universe,
Path-finder, road-builder,
Mediator, royal giver;
Rightly seeing, rightly seen,
Of joyful and transparent mien.
'T is a sparkle passing
From each to each, from thee to me,
To and fro perpetually;
Sharing all, daring all,
Levelling, displacing
Each obstruction, it unites
Equals remote, and seeming opposites.
And ever and forever Love
Delights to build a road:
Unheeded Danger near him strides,
Love laughs, and on a lion rides.
But Cupid wears another face,
Born into Daemons less divine:
His roses bleach apace,

His nectar smacks of wine.
The Daemon ever builds a wall,
Himself encloses and includes,
Solitude in solitudes:
In like sort his love doth fall.
He doth elect
The beautiful and fortunate,
And the sons of intellect,
And the souls of ample fate,
Who the Future's gates unbar, —
Minions of the Morning Star.
In his prowess he exults,
And the multitude insults.
His impatient looks devour
Oft the humble and the poor;
And, seeing his eye glare,
They drop their few pale flowers,
Gathered with hope to please,
Along the mountain towers, —
Lose courage, and despair.
He will never be gainsaid, —
Pitiless, will not be stayed;
His hot tyranny
Burns up every other tie.
Therefore comes an hour from Jove
Which his ruthless will defies,
And the dogs of Fate unties.
Shiver the palaces of glass;
Shrivel the rainbow-colored walls,
Where in bright Art each god and sibyl dwelt
Secure as in the zodiac's belt;
And the galleries and halls,

Wherein every siren sung,
Like a meteor pass.
For this fortune wanted root
In the core of God's abysm,—
Was a weed of self and schism;
And ever the Daemonic Love
Is the ancestor of wars
And the parent of remorse.

III
THE CELESTIAL LOVE

But God said,
'I will have a purer gift;
There is smoke in the flame;
New flowerets bring, new prayers uplift,
And love without a name.
Fond children, ye desire
To please each other well;
Another round, a higher,
Ye shall climb on the heavenly stair,
And selfish preference forbear;
And in right deserving,
And without a swerving
Each from your proper state,
Weave roses for your mate.

'Deep, deep are loving eyes,
Flowed with naphtha fiery sweet;
And the point is paradise,
Where their glances meet:
Their reach shall yet be more profound,
And a vision without bound:
The axis of those eyes sun-clear
Be the axis of the sphere:
So shall the lights ye pour amain
Go, without check or intervals,
Through from the empyrean walls
Unto the same again.'

Higher far into the pure realm,
Over sun and star,
Over the flickering Daemon film,
Thou must mount for love;
Into vision where all form
In one only form dissolves;
In a region where the wheel
On which all beings ride
Visibly revolves;
Where the starred, eternal worm
Girds the world with bound and term;
Where unlike things are like;
Where good and ill,
And joy and moan,
Melt into one.

There Past, Present, Future, shoot
Triple blossoms from one root;
Substances at base divided,
In their summits are united;
There the holy essence rolls,
One through separated souls;
And the sunny Aeon sleeps
Folding Nature in its deeps,
And every fair and every good,
Known in part, or known impure,
To men below,
In their archetypes endure.
The race of gods,
Or those we erring own,
Are shadows flitting up and down
In the still abodes.
The circles of that sea are laws
Which publish and which hide the cause.

Pray for a beam
Out of that sphere,
Thee to guide and to redeem.
O, what a load
Of care and toil,
By lying use bestowed,
From his shoulders falls who sees
The true astronomy,
The period of peace.
Counsel which the ages kept
Shall the well-born soul accept.
As the overhanging trees
Fill the lake with images,—
As garment draws the garment's hem,
Men their fortunes bring with them.
By right or wrong,
Lands and goods go to the strong.
Property will brutely draw
Still to the proprietor;
Silver to silver creep and wind,
And kind to kind.

Nor less the eternal poles
Of tendency distribute souls.
There need no vows to bind
Whom not each other seek, but find.
They give and take no pledge or oath,—
Nature is the bond of both:
No prayer persuades, no flattery fawns,—
Their noble meanings are their pawns.
Plain and cold is their address,
Power have they for tenderness;
And, so thoroughly is known
Each other's counsel by his own,

They can parley without meeting;
Need is none of forms of greeting;
They can well communicate
In their innermost estate;
When each the other shall avoid,
Shall each by each be most enjoyed.

Not with scarfs or perfumed gloves
Do these celebrate their loves:
Not by jewels, feasts and savors,
Not by ribbons or by favors,
But by the sun-spark on the sea,
And the cloud-shadow on the lea,
The soothing lapse of morn to mirk,
And the cheerful round of work.
Their cords of love so public are,
They intertwine the farthest star:
The throbbing sea, the quaking earth,
Yield sympathy and signs of mirth;
Is none so high, so mean is none,
But feels and seals this union;
Even the fell Furies are appeased,
The good applaud, the lost are eased.

Love's hearts are faithful, but not fond,
Bound for the just, but not beyond;
Not glad, as the low-loving herd,
Of self in other still preferred,
But they have heartily designed
The benefit of broad mankind.
And they serve men austerely,
After their own genius, clearly,
Without a false humility;
For this is Love's nobility, —

Not to scatter bread and gold,
Goods and raiment bought and sold;
But to hold fast his simple sense,
And speak the speech of innocence,
And with hand and body and blood,
To make his bosom-counsel good.
He that feeds men serveth few;
He serves all who dares be true.

THE APOLOGY

Think me not unkind and rude
That I walk alone in grove and glen;
I go to the god of the wood
To fetch his word to men.

Tax not my sloth that I
Fold my arms beside the brook;
Each cloud that floated in the sky
Writes a letter in my book.

Chide me not, laborious band,
For the idle flowers I brought;
Every aster in my hand
Goes home loaded with a thought.

There was never mystery
But 'tis figured in the flowers;
Was never secret history
But birds tell it in the bowers.

One harvest from thy field
Homeward brought the oxen strong;
A second crop thine acres yield,
Which I gather in a song.

MERLIN I

Thy trivial harp will never please
Or fill my craving ear;
Its chords should ring as blows the breeze,
Free, peremptory, clear.
No jingling serenader's art,
Nor tinkle of piano strings,
Can make the wild blood start
In its mystic springs.
The kingly bard
Must smite the chords rudely and hard,
As with hammer or with mace;
That they may render back
Artful thunder, which conveys
Secrets of the solar track,
Sparks of the supersolar blaze.
Merlin's blows are strokes of fate,
Chiming with the forest tone,
When boughs buffet boughs in the wood;
Chiming with the gasp and moan
Of the ice-imprisoned flood;
With the pulse of manly hearts;
With the voice of orators;
With the din of city arts;
With the cannonade of wars;
With the marches of the brave;
And prayers of might from martyrs' cave.

Great is the art,

Great be the manners, of the bard.
He shall not his brain encumber
With the coil of rhythm and number;
But, leaving rule and pale forethought,
He shall aye climb
For his rhyme.
'Pass in, pass in,' the angels say,
'In to the upper doors,
Nor count compartments of the floors,
But mount to paradise
By the stairway of surprise.'

Blameless master of the games,
King of sport that never shames,
He shall daily joy dispense
Hid in song's sweet influence.
Forms more cheerly live and go,
What time the subtle mind
Sings aloud the tune whereto
Their pulses beat,
And march their feet,
And their members are combined.

By Sybarites beguiled,
He shall no task decline;
Merlin's mighty line
Extremes of nature reconciled, —
Bereaved a tyrant of his will,
And made the lion mild.
Songs can the tempest still,
Scattered on the stormy air,
Mould the year to fair increase,
And bring in poetic peace.

He shall not seek to weave,
In weak, unhappy times,

Efficacious rhymes;
Wait his returning strength.
Bird that from the nadir's floor
To the zenith's top can soar,—
The soaring orbit of the muse exceeds that journey's length.
Nor profane affect to hit
Or compass that, by meddling wit,
Which only the propitious mind
Publishes when 't is inclined.
There are open hours
When the God's will sallies free,
And the dull idiot might see
The flowing fortunes of a thousand years;—
Sudden, at unawares,
Self-moved, fly-to the doors.
Nor sword of angels could reveal
What they conceal.

MERLIN II

The rhyme of the poet
Modulates the king's affairs;
Balance-loving Nature
Made all things in pairs.
To every foot its antipode;
Each color with its counter glowed;
To every tone beat answering tones,
Higher or graver;
Flavor gladly blends with flavor;
Leaf answers leaf upon the bough;
And match the paired cotyledons.
Hands to hands, and feet to feet,
In one body grooms and brides;
Eldest rite, two married sides
In every mortal meet.
Light's far furnace shines,
Smelting balls and bars,
Forging double stars,
Glittering twins and trines.
The animals are sick with love,
Lovesick with rhyme;
Each with all propitious Time
Into chorus wove.

Like the dancers' ordered band,
Thoughts come also hand in hand;
In equal couples mated,
Or else alternated;
Adding by their mutual gage,

One to other, health and age.
Solitary fancies go
Short-lived wandering to and fro,
Most like to bachelors,
Or an ungiven maid,
Not ancestors,
With no posterity to make the lie afraid,
Or keep truth undecayed.
Perfect-paired as eagle's wings,
Justice is the rhyme of things;
Trade and counting use
The self-same tuneful muse;
And Nemesis,
Who with even matches odd,
Who athwart space redresses
The partial wrong,
Fills the just period,
And finishes the song.

Subtle rhymes, with ruin rife,
Murmur in the house of life,
Sung by the Sisters as they spin;
In perfect time and measure they
Build and unbuild our echoing clay.
As the two twilights of the day
Fold us music-drunken in.

BACCHUS

Bring me wine, but wine which never grew
In the belly of the grape,
Or grew on vine whose tap-roots, reaching through,
Under the Andes to the Cape,
Suffer no savor of the earth to scape.

Let its grapes the morn salute
From a nocturnal root,
Which feels the acrid juice
Of Styx and Erebus;
And turns the woe of Night,
By its own craft, to a more rich delight.

We buy ashes for bread;
We buy diluted wine;
Give me of the true, —
Whose ample leaves and tendrils curled
Among the silver hills of heaven
Draw everlasting dew;
Wine of wine,
Blood of the world,
Form of forms, and mould of statures,
That I intoxicated,
And by the draught assimilated,
May float at pleasure through all natures;
The bird-language rightly spell,
And that which roses say so well.

Wine that is shed

Like the torrents of the sun
Up the horizon walls,
Or like the Atlantic streams, which run
When the South Sea calls.

Water and bread,
Food which needs no transmuting,
Rainbow-flowering, wisdom-fruiting,
Wine which is already man,
Food which teach and reason can.

Wine which Music is, —
Music and wine are one, —
That I, drinking this,
Shall hear far Chaos talk with me;
Kings unborn shall walk with me;
And the poor grass shall plot and plan
What it will do when it is man.
Quickened so, will I unlock
Every crypt of every rock.

I thank the joyful juice
For all I know; —
Winds of remembering
Of the ancient being blow,
And seeming-solid walls of use
Open and flow.

Pour, Bacchus! the remembering wine;
Retrieve the loss of me and mine!
Vine for vine be antidote,
And the grape requite the lote!
Haste to cure the old despair, —
Reason in Nature's lotus drenched,
The memory of ages quenched;
Give them again to shine;

Let wine repair what this undid;
And where the infection slid,
A dazzling memory revive;
Refresh the faded tints,
Recut the aged prints,
And write my old adventures with the pen
Which on the first day drew,
Upon the tablets blue,
The dancing Pleiads and eternal men.

MEROPS

What care I, so they stand the same,—
Things of the heavenly mind,—
How long the power to give them name
Tarries yet behind?

Thus far to-day your favors reach,
O fair, appeasing presences!
Ye taught my lips a single speech,
And a thousand silences.

Space grants beyond his fated road
No inch to the god of day;
And copious language still bestowed
One word, no more, to say.

THE HOUSE

There is no architect
Can build as the Muse can;
She is skilful to select
Materials for her plan;

Slow and warily to choose
Rafters of immortal pine,
Or cedar incorruptible,
Worthy her design,

She threads dark Alpine forests
Or valleys by the sea,
In many lands, with painful steps,
Ere she can find a tree.

She ransacks mines and ledges
And quarries every rock,
To hew the famous adamant
For each eternal block—

She lays her beams in music,
In music every one,
To the cadence of the whirling world
Which dances round the sun—

That so they shall not be displaced
By lapses or by wars,
But for the love of happy souls
Outlive the newest stars.

SAADI

Trees in groves,
Kine in droves,
In ocean sport the scaly herds,
Wedge-like cleave the air the birds,
To northern lakes fly wind-borne ducks,
Browse the mountain sheep in flocks,
Men consort in camp and town,
But the poet dwells alone.

God, who gave to him the lyre,
Of all mortals the desire,
For all breathing men's behoof,
Straitly charged him, 'Sit aloof;'
Annexed a warning, poets say,
To the bright premium, —
Ever, when twain together play,
Shall the harp be dumb.

Many may come,
But one shall sing;
Two touch the string,
The harp is dumb.
Though there come a million,
Wise Saadi dwells alone.

Yet Saadi loved the race of men, —
No churl, immured in cave or den;
In bower and hall
He wants them all,
Nor can dispense

With Persia for his audience;
They must give ear,
Grow red with joy and white with fear;
But he has no companion;
Come ten, or come a million,
Good Saadi dwells alone.

Be thou ware where Saadi dwells;
Wisdom of the gods is he, —
Entertain it reverently.
Gladly round that golden lamp
Sylvan deities encamp,
And simple maids and noble youth
Are welcome to the man of truth.
Most welcome they who need him most,
They feed the spring which they exhaust;
For greater need
Draws better deed:
But, critic, spare thy vanity,
Nor show thy pompous parts,
To vex with odious subtlety
The cheerer of men's hearts.

Sad-eyed Fakirs swiftly say
Endless dirges to decay,
Never in the blaze of light
Lose the shudder of midnight;
Pale at overflowing noon
Hear wolves barking at the moon;
In the bower of dalliance sweet
Hear the far Avenger's feet:
And shake before those awful Powers,
Who in their pride forgive not ours.
Thus the sad-eyed Fakirs preach:
'Bard, when thee would Allah teach,

And lift thee to his holy mount,
He sends thee from his bitter fount
Wormwood,—saying, "Go thy ways;
Drink not the Malaga of praise,
But do the deed thy fellows hate,
And compromise thy peaceful state;
Smite the white breasts which thee fed.
Stuff sharp thorns beneath the head
Of them thou shouldst have comforted;
For out of woe and out of crime
Draws the heart a lore sublime."'
And yet it seemeth not to me
That the high gods love tragedy;
For Saadi sat in the sun,
And thanks was his contrition;
For haircloth and for bloody whips,
Had active hands and smiling lips;
And yet his runes he rightly read,
And to his folk his message sped.
Sunshine in his heart transferred
Lighted each transparent word,
And well could honoring Persia learn
What Saadi wished to say;
For Saadi's nightly stars did burn
Brighter than Jami's day.

Whispered the Muse in Saadi's cot:
'O gentle Saadi, listen not,
Tempted by thy praise of wit,
Or by thirst and appetite
For the talents not thine own,
To sons of contradiction.
Never, son of eastern morning,
Follow falsehood, follow scorning.
Denounce who will, who will deny,

And pile the hills to scale the sky;
Let theist, atheist, pantheist,
Define and wrangle how they list,
Fierce conserver, fierce destroyer,—
But thou, joy-giver and enjoyer,
Unknowing war, unknowing crime,
Gentle Saadi, mind thy rhyme;
Heed not what the brawlers say,
Heed thou only Saadi's lay.

'Let the great world bustle on
With war and trade, with camp and town;
A thousand men shall dig and eat;
At forge and furnace thousands sweat;
And thousands sail the purple sea,
And give or take the stroke of war,
Or crowd the market and bazaar;
Oft shall war end, and peace return,
And cities rise where cities burn,
Ere one man my hill shall climb,
Who can turn the golden rhyme.
Let them manage how they may,
Heed thou only Saadi's lay.
Seek the living among the dead,—
Man in man is imprisonèd;
Barefooted Dervish is not poor,
If fate unlock his bosom's door,
So that what his eye hath seen
His tongue can paint as bright, as keen;
And what his tender heart hath felt
With equal fire thy heart shalt melt.
For, whom the Muses smile upon,
And touch with soft persuasion,
His words like a storm-wind can bring
Terror and beauty on their wing;

In his every syllable
Lurketh Nature veritable;
And though he speak in midnight dark, —
In heaven no star, on earth no spark, —
Yet before the listener's eye
Swims the world in ecstasy,
The forest waves, the morning breaks,
The pastures sleep, ripple the lakes,
Leaves twinkle, flowers like persons be,
And life pulsates in rock or tree.
Saadi, so far thy words shall reach:
Suns rise and set in Saadi's speech!'

And thus to Saadi said the Muse:
'Eat thou the bread which men refuse;
Flee from the goods which from thee flee;
Seek nothing, —Fortune seeketh thee.
Nor mount, nor dive; all good things keep
The midway of the eternal deep.
Wish not to fill the isles with eyes
To fetch thee birds of paradise:
On thine orchard's edge belong
All the brags of plume and song;
Wise Ali's sunbright sayings pass
For proverbs in the market-place:
Through mountains bored by regal art,
Toil whistles as he drives his cart.
Nor scour the seas, nor sift mankind,
A poet or a friend to find:
Behold, he watches at the door!
Behold his shadow on the floor!
Open innumerable doors
The heaven where unveiled Allah pours
The flood of truth, the flood of good,
The Seraph's and the Cherub's food.

Those doors are men: the Pariah hind
Admits thee to the perfect Mind.
Seek not beyond thy cottage wall
Redeemers that can yield thee all:
While thou sittest at thy door
On the desert's yellow floor,
Listening to the gray-haired crones,
Foolish gossips, ancient drones,
Saadi, see! they rise in stature
To the height of mighty Nature,
And the secret stands revealed
Fraudulent Time in vain concealed, —
That blessed gods in servile masks
Plied for thee thy household tasks.'

HOLIDAYS

From fall to spring, the russet acorn,
Fruit beloved of maid and boy,
Lent itself beneath the forest,
To be the children's toy.

Pluck it now! In vain,—thou canst not;
Its root has pierced yon shady mound;
Toy no longer—it has duties;
It is anchored in the ground.

Year by year the rose-lipped maiden,
Playfellow of young and old,
Was frolic sunshine, dear to all men,
More dear to one than mines of gold.

Whither went the lovely hoyden?
Disappeared in blessed wife;
Servant to a wooden cradle,
Living in a baby's life.

Still thou playest;—short vacation
Fate grants each to stand aside;
Now must thou be man and artist,—
'T is the turning of the tide.

XENOPHANES

By fate, not option, frugal Nature gave
One scent to hyson and to wall-flower,
One sound to pine-groves and to waterfalls,
One aspect to the desert and the lake.
It was her stern necessity: all things
Are of one pattern made; bird, beast and flower,
Song, picture, form, space, thought and character
Deceive us, seeming to be many things,
And are but one. Beheld far off, they part
As God and devil; bring them to the mind,
They dull its edge with their monotony.
To know one element, explore another,
And in the second reappears the first.
The specious panorama of a year
But multiplies the image of a day,—
A belt of mirrors round a taper's flame;
And universal Nature, through her vast
And crowded whole, an infinite paroquet,
Repeats one note.

THE DAY'S RATION

When I was born,
From all the seas of strength Fate filled a chalice,
Saying, 'This be thy portion, child; this chalice,
Less than a lily's, thou shalt daily draw
From my great arteries,—nor less, nor more.'
All substances the cunning chemist Time
Melts down into that liquor of my life,—
Friends, foes, joys, fortunes, beauty and disgust.
And whether I am angry or content,
Indebted or insulted, loved or hurt,
All he distils into sidereal wine
And brims my little cup; heedless, alas!
Of all he sheds how little it will hold,
How much runs over on the desert sands.
If a new Muse draw me with splendid ray,
And I uplift myself into its heaven,
The needs of the first sight absorb my blood,
And all the following hours of the day
Drag a ridiculous age.
To-day, when friends approach, and every hour
Brings book, or starbright scroll of genius,
The little cup will hold not a bead more,
And all the costly liquor runs to waste;
Nor gives the jealous lord one diamond drop
So to be husbanded for poorer days.
Why need I volumes, if one word suffice?
Why need I galleries, when a pupil's draught

After the master's sketch fills and o'erfills
My apprehension? Why seek Italy,
Who cannot circumnavigate the sea
Of thoughts and things at home, but still adjourn
The nearest matters for a thousand days?

BLIGHT

Give me truths;
For I am weary of the surfaces,
And die of inanition. If I knew
Only the herbs and simples of the wood,
Rue, cinquefoil, gill, vervain and agrimony,
Blue-vetch and trillium, hawkweed, sassafras,
Milkweeds and murky brakes, quaint pipes and sundew,
And rare and virtuous roots, which in these woods
Draw untold juices from the common earth,
Untold, unknown, and I could surely spell
Their fragrance, and their chemistry apply
By sweet affinities to human flesh,
Driving the foe and stablishing the friend, —
O, that were much, and I could be a part
Of the round day, related to the sun
And planted world, and full executor
Of their imperfect functions.
But these young scholars, who invade our hills,
Bold as the engineer who fells the wood,
And travelling often in the cut he makes,
Love not the flower they pluck, and know it not,
And all their botany is Latin names.
The old men studied magic in the flowers,
And human fortunes in astronomy,
And an omnipotence in chemistry,
Preferring things to names, for these were men,
Were unitarians of the united world,
And, wheresoever their clear eye-beams fell,

They caught the footsteps of the SAME. Our eyes
Are armed, but we are strangers to the stars,
And strangers to the mystic beast and bird,
And strangers to the plant and to the mine.
The injured elements say, 'Not in us;'
And night and day, ocean and continent,
Fire, plant and mineral say, 'Not in us;'
And haughtily return us stare for stare.
For we invade them impiously for gain;
We devastate them unreligiously,
And coldly ask their pottage, not their love.
Therefore they shove us from them, yield to us
Only what to our griping toil is due;
But the sweet affluence of love and song,
The rich results of the divine consents
Of man and earth, of world beloved and lover,
The nectar and ambrosia, are withheld;
And in the midst of spoils and slaves, we thieves
And pirates of the universe, shut out
Daily to a more thin and outward rind,
Turn pale and starve. Therefore, to our sick eyes,
The stunted trees look sick, the summer short,
Clouds shade the sun, which will not tan our hay,
And nothing thrives to reach its natural term;
And life, shorn of its venerable length,
Even at its greatest space is a defeat,
And dies in anger that it was a dupe;
And, in its highest noon and wantonness,
Is early frugal, like a beggar's child;
Even in the hot pursuit of the best aims
And prizes of ambition, checks its hand,
Like Alpine cataracts frozen as they leaped,
Chilled with a miserly comparison
Of the toy's purchase with the length of life.

MUSKETAQUID

Because I was content with these poor fields,
Low, open meads, slender and sluggish streams,
And found a home in haunts which others scorned,
The partial wood-gods overpaid my love,
And granted me the freedom of their state,
And in their secret senate have prevailed
With the dear, dangerous lords that rule our life,
Made moon and planets parties to their bond,
And through my rock-like, solitary wont
Shot million rays of thought and tenderness.
For me, in showers, in sweeping showers, the Spring
Visits the valley;—break away the clouds,—
I bathe in the morn's soft and silvered air,
And loiter willing by yon loitering stream.
Sparrows far off, and nearer, April's bird,
Blue-coated,—flying before from tree to tree,
Courageous sing a delicate overture
To lead the tardy concert of the year.
Onward and nearer rides the sun of May;
And wide around, the marriage of the plants
Is sweetly solemnized. Then flows amain
The surge of summer's beauty; dell and crag,
Hollow and lake, hillside and pine arcade,
Are touched with genius. Yonder ragged cliff
Has thousand faces in a thousand hours.

Beneath low hills, in the broad interval
Through which at will our Indian rivulet
Winds mindful still of sannup and of squaw,

Whose pipe and arrow oft the plough unburies,
Here in pine houses built of new-fallen trees,
Supplanters of the tribe, the farmers dwell.
Traveller, to thee, perchance, a tedious road,
Or, it may be, a picture; to these men,
The landscape is an armory of powers,
Which, one by one, they know to draw and use.
They harness beast, bird, insect, to their work;
They prove the virtues of each bed of rock,
And, like the chemist 'mid his loaded jars,
Draw from each stratum its adapted use
To drug their crops or weapon their arts withal.
They turn the frost upon their chemic heap,
They set the wind to winnow pulse and grain,
They thank the spring-flood for its fertile slime,
And, on cheap summit-levels of the snow,
Slide with the sledge to inaccessible woods
O'er meadows bottomless. So, year by year,
They fight the elements with elements
(That one would say, meadow and forest walked,
Transmuted in these men to rule their like),
And by the order in the field disclose
The order regnant in the yeoman's brain.

What these strong masters wrote at large in miles,
I followed in small copy in my acre;
For there's no rood has not a star above it;
The cordial quality of pear or plum
Ascends as gladly in a single tree
As in broad orchards resonant with bees;
And every atom poises for itself,
And for the whole. The gentle deities
Showed me the lore of colors and of sounds,
The innumerable tenements of beauty.
The miracle of generative force,

Far-reaching concords of astronomy
Felt in the plants and in the punctual birds;
Better, the linked purpose of the whole,
And, chiefest prize, found I true liberty
In the glad home plain-dealing Nature gave.
The polite found me impolite; the great
Would mortify me, but in vain; for still
I am a willow of the wilderness,
Loving the wind that bent me. All my hurts
My garden spade can heal. A woodland walk,
A quest of river-grapes, a mocking thrush,
A wild-rose, or rock-loving columbine,
Salve my worst wounds.
For thus the wood-gods murmured in my ear:
'Dost love our manners? Canst thou silent lie?
Canst thou, thy pride forgot, like Nature pass
Into the winter night's extinguished mood?
Canst thou shine now, then darkle,
And being latent, feel thyself no less?
As, when the all-worshipped moon attracts the eye,
The river, hill, stems, foliage are obscure,
Yet envies none, none are unenviable.'

DIRGE

CONCORD, 1838

I reached the middle of the mount
Up which the incarnate soul must climb,
And paused for them, and looked around,
With me who walked through space and time.

Five rosy boys with morning light
Had leaped from one fair mother's arms,
Fronted the sun with hope as bright,
And greeted God with childhood's psalms.

Knows he who tills this lonely field
To reap its scanty corn,
What mystic fruit his acres yield
At midnight and at morn?

In the long sunny afternoon
The plain was full of ghosts;
I wandered up, I wandered down,
Beset by pensive hosts.

The winding Concord gleamed below,
Pouring as wide a flood
As when my brothers, long ago,
Came with me to the wood.

But they are gone, — the holy ones
Who trod with me this lovely vale;
The strong, star-bright companions
Are silent, low and pale.

My good, my noble, in their prime,
Who made this world the feast it was
Who learned with me the lore of time,
Who loved this dwelling-place!

They took this valley for their toy,
They played with it in every mood;
A cell for prayer, a hall for joy,—
They treated Nature as they would.

They colored the horizon round;
Stars flamed and faded as they bade,
All echoes hearkened for their sound,—
They made the woodlands glad or mad.

I touch this flower of silken leaf,
Which once our childhood knew;
Its soft leaves wound me with a grief
Whose balsam never grew.

Hearken to yon pine-warbler
Singing aloft in the tree!
Hearest thou, O traveller,
What he singeth to me?

Not unless God made sharp thine ear
With sorrow such as mine,
Out of that delicate lay could'st thou
Its heavy tale divine.

'Go, lonely man,' it saith;
'They loved thee from their birth;
Their hands were pure, and pure their faith,—
There are no such hearts on earth.

'Ye drew one mother's milk,
One chamber held ye all;

A very tender history
Did in your childhood fall.

'You cannot unlock your heart,
The key is gone with them;
The silent organ loudest chants
The master's requiem.'

THRENODY

The South-wind brings
Life, sunshine and desire,
And on every mount and meadow
Breathes aromatic fire;
But over the dead he has no power,
The lost, the lost, he cannot restore;
And, looking over the hills, I mourn
The darling who shall not return.

I see my empty house,
I see my trees repair their boughs;
And he, the wondrous child,
Whose silver warble wild
Outvalued every pulsing sound
Within the air's cerulean round, —
The hyacinthine boy, for whom
Morn well might break and April bloom,
The gracious boy, who did adorn
The world whereinto he was born,
And by his countenance repay
The favor of the loving Day, —
Has disappeared from the Day's eye;
Far and wide she cannot find him;
My hopes pursue, they cannot bind him.
Returned this day, the South-wind searches,
And finds young pines and budding birches;
But finds not the budding man;
Nature, who lost, cannot remake him;

Fate let him fall, Fate can't retake him;
Nature, Fate, men, him seek in vain.

And whither now, my truant wise and sweet,
O, whither tend thy feet?
I had the right, few days ago,
Thy steps to watch, thy place to know:
How have I forfeited the right?
Hast thou forgot me in a new delight?
I hearken for thy household cheer,
O eloquent child!
Whose voice, an equal messenger,
Conveyed thy meaning mild.
What though the pains and joys
Whereof it spoke were toys
Fitting his age and ken,
Yet fairest dames and bearded men,
Who heard the sweet request,
So gentle, wise and grave,
Bended with joy to his behest
And let the world's affairs go by,
A while to share his cordial game,
Or mend his wicker wagon-frame,
Still plotting how their hungry fear
That winsome voice again might hear;
For his lips could well pronounce
Words that were persuasions.

Gentlest guardians marked serene
His early hope, his liberal mien;
Took counsel from his guiding eyes
To make this wisdom earthly wise.
Ah, vainly do these eyes recall
The school-march, each day's festival,
When every morn my bosom glowed

To watch the convoy on the road;
The babe in willow wagon closed,
With rolling eyes and face composed;
With children forward and behind,
Like Cupids studiously inclined;
And he the chieftain paced beside,
The centre of the troop allied,
With sunny face of sweet repose,
To guard the babe from fancied foes.
The little captain innocent
Took the eye with him as he went;
Each village senior paused to scan
And speak the lovely caravan.
From the window I look out
To mark thy beautiful parade,
Stately marching in cap and coat
To some tune by fairies played;—
A music heard by thee alone
To works as noble led thee on.

Now Love and Pride, alas! in vain,
Up and down their glances strain.
The painted sled stands where it stood;
The kennel by the corded wood;
His gathered sticks to stanch the wall
Of the snow-tower, when snow should fall;
The ominous hole he dug in the sand,
And childhood's castles built or planned;
His daily haunts I well discern,—
The poultry-yard, the shed, the barn,—
And every inch of garden ground
Paced by the blessed feet around,
From the roadside to the brook
Whereinto he loved to look.
Step the meek fowls where erst they ranged;

The wintry garden lies unchanged;
The brook into the stream runs on;
But the deep-eyed boy is gone.

On that shaded day,
Dark with more clouds than tempests are,
When thou didst yield thy innocent breath
In birdlike heavings unto death,
Night came, and Nature had not thee;
I said, 'We are mates in misery.'
The morrow dawned with needless glow;
Each snowbird chirped, each fowl must crow;
Each tramper started; but the feet
Of the most beautiful and sweet
Of human youth had left the hill
And garden,—they were bound and still.
There's not a sparrow or a wren,
There's not a blade of autumn grain,
Which the four seasons do not tend
And tides of life and increase lend;
And every chick of every bird,
And weed and rock-moss is preferred.
O ostrich-like forgetfulness!
O loss of larger in the less!
Was there no star that could be sent,
No watcher in the firmament,
No angel from the countless host
That loiters round the crystal coast,
Could stoop to heal that only child,
Nature's sweet marvel undefiled,
And keep the blossom of the earth,
Which all her harvests were not worth?
Not mine,—I never called thee mine,
But Nature's heir,—if I repine,
And seeing rashly torn and moved

Not what I made, but what I loved,
Grow early old with grief that thou
Must to the wastes of Nature go, —
'T is because a general hope
Was quenched, and all must doubt and grope.
For flattering planets seemed to say
This child should ills of ages stay,
By wondrous tongue, and guided pen,
Bring the flown Muses back to men.
Perchance not he but Nature ailed,
The world and not the infant failed.
It was not ripe yet to sustain
A genius of so fine a strain,
Who gazed upon the sun and moon
As if he came unto his own,
And, pregnant with his grander thought,
Brought the old order into doubt.
His beauty once their beauty tried;
They could not feed him, and he died,
And wandered backward as in scorn,
To wait an aeon to be born.
Ill day which made this beauty waste,
Plight broken, this high face defaced!
Some went and came about the dead;
And some in books of solace read;
Some to their friends the tidings say;
Some went to write, some went to pray;
One tarried here, there hurried one;
But their heart abode with none.
Covetous death bereaved us all,
To aggrandize one funeral.
The eager fate which carried thee
Took the largest part of me:
For this losing is true dying;

This is lordly man's down-lying,
This his slow but sure reclining,
Star by star his world resigning.

O child of paradise,
Boy who made dear his father's home,
In whose deep eyes
Men read the welfare of the times to come,
I am too much bereft.
The world dishonored thou hast left.
O truth's and nature's costly lie!
O trusted broken prophecy!
O richest fortune sourly crossed!
Born for the future, to the future lost!

The deep Heart answered, 'Weepest thou?
Worthier cause for passion wild
If I had not taken the child.
And deemest thou as those who pore,
With aged eyes, short way before, —
Think'st Beauty vanished from the coast
Of matter, and thy darling lost?
Taught he not thee — the man of eld,
Whose eyes within his eyes beheld
Heaven's numerous hierarchy span
The mystic gulf from God to man?
To be alone wilt thou begin
When worlds of lovers hem thee in?
To-morrow, when the masks shall fall
That dizen Nature's carnival,
The pure shall see by their own will,
Which overflowing Love shall fill,
'T is not within the force of fate
The fate-conjoined to separate.
But thou, my votary, weepest thou?

I gave thee sight—where is it now?
I taught thy heart beyond the reach
Of ritual, bible, or of speech;
Wrote in thy mind's transparent table,
As far as the incommunicable;
Taught thee each private sign to raise
Lit by the supersolar blaze.
Past utterance, and past belief,
And past the blasphemy of grief,
The mysteries of Nature's heart;
And though no Muse can these impart,
Throb thine with Nature's throbbing breast,
And all is clear from east to west.

'I came to thee as to a friend;
Dearest, to thee I did not send
Tutors, but a joyful eye,
Innocence that matched the sky,
Lovely locks, a form of wonder,
Laughter rich as woodland thunder,
That thou might'st entertain apart
The richest flowering of all art:
And, as the great all-loving Day
Through smallest chambers takes its way,
That thou might'st break thy daily bread
With prophet, savior and head;
That thou might'st cherish for thine own
The riches of sweet Mary's Son,
Boy-Rabbi, Israel's paragon.
And thoughtest thou such guest
Would in thy hall take up his rest?
Would rushing life forget her laws,
Fate's glowing revolution pause?
High omens ask diviner guess;
Not to be conned to tediousness

And know my higher gifts unbind
The zone that girds the incarnate mind.
When the scanty shores are full
With Thought's perilous, whirling pool;
When frail Nature can no more,
Then the Spirit strikes the hour:
My servant Death, with solving rite,
Pours finite into infinite.
Wilt thou freeze love's tidal flow,
Whose streams through Nature circling go?
Nail the wild star to its track
On the half-climbed zodiac?
Light is light which radiates,
Blood is blood which circulates,
Life is life which generates,
And many-seeming life is one, —
Wilt thou transfix and make it none?
Its onward force too starkly pent
In figure, bone and lineament?
Wilt thou, uncalled, interrogate,
Talker! the unreplying Fate?
Nor see the genius of the whole
Ascendant in the private soul,
Beckon it when to go and come,
Self-announced its hour of doom?
Fair the soul's recess and shrine,
Magic-built to last a season;
Masterpiece of love benign,
Fairer that expansive reason
Whose omen 'tis, and sign.
Wilt thou not ope thy heart to know
What rainbows teach, and sunsets show?
Verdict which accumulates
From lengthening scroll of human fates,

Voice of earth to earth returned,
Prayers of saints that inly burned,—
Saying, *What is excellent,*
As God lives, is permanent;
Hearts are dust, hearts' loves remain;
Heart's love will meet thee again.
Revere the Maker; fetch thine eye
Up to his style, and manners of the sky.
Not of adamant and gold
Built he heaven stark and cold;
No, but a nest of bending reeds,
Flowering grass and scented weeds;
Or like a traveller's fleeing tent,
Or bow above the tempest bent;
Built of tears and sacred flames,
And virtue reaching to its aims;
Built of furtherance and pursuing,
Not of spent deeds, but of doing.
Silent rushes the swift Lord
Through ruined systems still restored,
Broadsowing, bleak and void to bless,
Plants with worlds the wilderness;
Waters with tears of ancient sorrow
Apples of Eden ripe to-morrow.
House and tenant go to ground,
Lost in God, in Godhead found.'

CONCORD HYMN

SUNG AT THE COMPLETION OF THE BATTLE
MONUMENT, JULY 4, 1837

By the rude bridge that arched the flood,
Their flag to April's breeze unfurled,
Here once the embattled farmers stood
And fired the shot heard round the world.

The foe long since in silence slept;
Alike the conqueror silent sleeps;
And Time the ruined bridge has swept
Down the dark stream which seaward creeps.

On this green bank, by this soft stream,
We set to-day a votive stone;
That memory may their deed redeem,
When, like our sires, our sons are gone.

Spirit, that made those heroes dare
To die, and leave their children free,
Bid Time and Nature gently spare
The shaft we raise to them and thee.

II
MAY-DAY AND OTHER PIECES

MAY-DAY

Daughter of Heaven and Earth, coy Spring,
With sudden passion languishing,
Teaching Barren moors to smile,
Painting pictures mile on mile,
Holds a cup with cowslip-wreaths,
Whence a smokeless incense breathes.
The air is full of whistlings bland;
What was that I heard
Out of the hazy land?
Harp of the wind, or song of bird,
Or vagrant booming of the air,
Voice of a meteor lost in day?
Such tidings of the starry sphere
Can this elastic air convey.
Or haply 'twas the cannonade
Of the pent and darkened lake,
Cooled by the pendent mountain's shade,
Whose deeps, till beams of noonday break,
Afflicted moan, and latest hold
Even into May the iceberg cold.
Was it a squirrel's pettish bark,
Or clarionet of jay? or hark
Where yon wedged line the Nestor leads,

Steering north with raucous cry
Through tracts and provinces of sky,
Every night alighting down
In new landscapes of romance,

Where darkling feed the clamorous clans
By lonely lakes to men unknown.
Come the tumult whence it will,
Voice of sport, or rush of wings,
It is a sound, it is a token
That the marble sleep is broken,
And a change has passed on things.

When late I walked, in earlier days,
All was stiff and stark;
Knee-deep snows choked all the ways,
In the sky no spark;
Firm-braced I sought my ancient woods,
Struggling through the drifted roads;
The whited desert knew me not,
Snow-ridges masked each darling spot;
The summer dells, by genius haunted,
One arctic moon had disenchanted.
All the sweet secrets therein hid
By Fancy, ghastly spells undid.
Eldest mason, Frost, had piled
Swift cathedrals in the wild;
The piny hosts were sheeted ghosts
In the star-lit minster aisled.
I found no joy: the icy wind
Might rule the forest to his mind.
Who would freeze on frozen lakes?
Back to books and sheltered home,
And wood-fire flickering on the walls,
To hear, when, 'mid our talk and games,

Without the baffled North-wind calls.
But soft! a sultry morning breaks;
The ground-pines wash their rusty green,
The maple-tops their crimson tint,
On the soft path each track is seen,
The girl's foot leaves its neater print.
The pebble loosened from the frost
Asks of the urchin to be tost.
In flint and marble beats a heart,
The kind Earth takes her children's part,
The green lane is the school-boy's friend,
Low leaves his quarrel apprehend,
The fresh ground loves his top and ball,
The air rings jocund to his call,
The brimming brook invites a leap,
He dives the hollow, climbs the steep.
The youth sees omens where he goes,
And speaks all languages the rose,
The wood-fly mocks with tiny voice
The far halloo of human voice;
The perfumed berry on the spray
Smacks of faint memories far away.
A subtle chain of countless rings
The next into the farthest brings,
And, striving to be man, the worm
Mounts through all the spires of form.

The caged linnet in the Spring
Hearkens for the choral glee,
When his fellows on the wing
Migrate from the Southern Sea;
When trellised grapes their flowers unmask,
And the new-born tendrils twine,
The old wine darkling in the cask
Feels the bloom on the living vine,

And bursts the hoops at hint of Spring:
And so, perchance, in Adam's race,
Of Eden's bower some dream-like trace
Survived the Flight and swam the Flood,
And wakes the wish in youngest blood
To tread the forfeit Paradise,
And feed once more the exile's eyes;
And ever when the happy child
In May beholds the blooming wild,
And hears in heaven the bluebird sing,
'Onward,' he cries, 'your baskets bring,—
In the next field is air more mild,
And o'er yon hazy crest is Eden's balmier spring.'

Not for a regiment's parade,
Nor evil laws or rulers made,
Blue Walden rolls its cannonade,
But for a lofty sign
Which the Zodiac threw,
That the bondage-days are told.
And waters free as winds shall flow.
Lo! how all the tribes combine
To rout the flying foe.
See, every patriot oak-leaf throws
His elfin length upon the snows,
Not idle, since the leaf all day
Draws to the spot the solar ray,
Ere sunset quarrying inches down,
And halfway to the mosses brown;
While the grass beneath the rime
Has hints of the propitious time,
And upward pries and perforates
Through the cold slab a thousand gates,
Till green lances peering through
Bend happy in the welkin blue.

As we thaw frozen flesh with snow,
So Spring will not her time forerun,
Mix polar night with tropic glow,
Nor cloy us with unshaded sun,
Nor wanton skip with bacchic dance,
But she has the temperance
Of the gods, whereof she is one, —
Masks her treasury of heat
Under east winds crossed with sleet.
Plants and birds and humble creatures
Well accept her rule austere;
Titan-born, to hardy natures
Cold is genial and dear.
As Southern wrath to Northern right
Is but straw to anthracite;
As in the day of sacrifice,
When heroes piled the pyre,
The dismal Massachusetts ice
Burned more than others' fire,
So Spring guards with surface cold
The garnered heat of ages old.
Hers to sow the seed of bread,
That man and all the kinds be fed;
And, when the sunlight fills the hours,
Dissolves the crust, displays the flowers.

Beneath the calm, within the light,
A hid unruly appetite
Of swifter life, a surer hope,
Strains every sense to larger scope,
Impatient to anticipate
The halting steps of aged Fate.
Slow grows the palm, too slow the pearl:
When Nature falters, fain would zeal
Grasp the felloes of her wheel,

And grasping give the orbs another whirl.
Turn swiftlier round, O tardy ball!
And sun this frozen side.
Bring hither back the robin's call,
Bring back the tulip's pride.

Why chidest thou the tardy Spring?
The hardy bunting does not chide;
The blackbirds make the maples ring
With social cheer and jubilee;
The redwing flutes his *o-ka-lee*,
The robins know the melting snow;
The sparrow meek, prophetic-eyed,
Her nest beside the snow-drift weaves,
Secure the osier yet will hide
Her callow brood in mantling leaves, —
And thou, by science all undone,
Why only must thy reason fail
To see the southing of the sun?

The world rolls round, — mistrust it not, —
Befalls again what once befell;
All things return, both sphere and mote,
And I shall hear my bluebird's note,
And dream the dream of Auburn dell.

April cold with dropping rain
Willows and lilacs brings again,
The whistle of returning birds,
And trumpet-lowing of the herds.
The scarlet maple-keys betray
What potent blood hath modest May,
What fiery force the earth renews,
The wealth of forms, the flush of hues;
What joy in rosy waves outpoured
Flows from the heart of Love, the Lord.

Hither rolls the storm of heat;
I feel its finer billows beat
Like a sea which me infolds;
Heat with viewless fingers moulds,
Swells, and mellows, and matures,
Paints, and flavors, and allures,
Bird and brier inly warms,
Still enriches and transforms,
Gives the reed and lily length,
Adds to oak and oxen strength,
Transforming what it doth infold,
Life out of death, new out of old,
Painting fawns' and leopards' fells,
Seethes the gulf-encrimsoning shells,
Fires gardens with a joyful blaze
Of tulips, in the morning's rays.
The dead log touched bursts into leaf,
The wheat-blade whispers of the sheaf.
What god is this imperial Heat,
Earth's prime secret, sculpture's seat?
Doth it bear hidden in its heart
Water-line patterns of all art?
Is it Daedalus? is it Love?
Or walks in mask almighty Jove,
And drops from Power's redundant horn
All seeds of beauty to be born?

Where shall we keep the holiday,
And duly greet the entering May?
Too strait and low our cottage doors,
And all unmeet our carpet floors;
Nor spacious court, nor monarch's hall,
Suffice to hold the festival.
Up and away! where haughty woods
Front the liberated floods:

We will climb the broad-backed hills,
Hear the uproar of their joy;
We will mark the leaps and gleams
Of the new-delivered streams,
And the murmuring rivers of sap
Mount in the pipes of the trees,
Giddy with day, to the topmost spire,
Which for a spike of tender green
Bartered its powdery cap;
And the colors of joy in the bird,
And the love in its carol heard,
Frog and lizard in holiday coats,
And turtle brave in his golden spots;
While cheerful cries of crag and plain
Reply to the thunder of river and main.

As poured the flood of the ancient sea
Spilling over mountain chains,
Bending forests as bends the sedge,
Faster flowing o'er the plains, —
A world-wide wave with a foaming edge
That rims the running silver sheet, —
So pours the deluge of the heat
Broad northward o'er the land,
Painting artless paradises,
Drugging herbs with Syrian spices,
Fanning secret fires which glow
In columbine and clover-blow,
Climbing the northern zones,
Where a thousand pallid towns
Lie like cockles by the main,
Or tented armies on a plain.
The million-handed sculptor moulds
Quaintest bud and blossom folds,
The million-handed painter pours

Opal hues and purple dye;
Azaleas flush the island floors,
And the tints of heaven reply.

Wreaths for the May! for happy Spring
To-day shall all her dowry bring,
The love of kind, the joy, the grace,
Hymen of element and race,
Knowing well to celebrate
With song and hue and star and state,
With tender light and youthful cheer,
The spousals of the new-born year.

Spring is strong and virtuous,
Broad-sowing, cheerful, plenteous,
Quickening underneath the mould
Grains beyond the price of gold.
So deep and large her bounties are,
That one broad, long midsummer day
Shall to the planet overpay
The ravage of a year of war.

Drug the cup, thou butler sweet,
And send the nectar round;
The feet that slid so long on sleet
Are glad to feel the ground.
Fill and saturate each kind
With good according to its mind,
Fill each kind and saturate
With good agreeing with its fate,
And soft perfection of its plan—
Willow and violet, maiden and man.

The bitter-sweet, the haunting air
Creepeth, bloweth everywhere;
It preys on all, all prey on it.

Blooms in beauty, thinks in wit,
Stings the strong with enterprise,
Makes travellers long for Indian skies,
And where it comes this courier fleet
Fans in all hearts expectance sweet,
As if to-morrow should redeem
The vanished rose of evening's dream.
By houses lies a fresher green,
On men and maids a ruddier mien,
As if Time brought a new relay
Of shining virgins every May,
And Summer came to ripen maids
To a beauty that not fades.

I saw the bud-crowned Spring go forth,
Stepping daily onward north
To greet staid ancient cavaliers
Filing single in stately train.
And who, and who are the travellers?
They were Night and Day, and Day and Night,
Pilgrims wight with step forthright.
I saw the Days deformed and low,
Short and bent by cold and snow;
The merry Spring threw wreaths on them,
Flower-wreaths gay with bud and bell;
Many a flower and many a gem,
They were refreshed by the smell,
They shook the snow from hats and shoon,
They put their April raiment on;
And those eternal forms,
Unhurt by a thousand storms,
Shot up to the height of the sky again,
And danced as merrily as young men.
I saw them mask their awful glance
Sidewise meek in gossamer lids;

And to speak my thought if none forbids
It was as if the eternal gods,
Tired of their starry periods,
Hid their majesty in cloth
Woven of tulips and painted moth.
On carpets green the maskers march
Below May's well-appointed arch,
Each star, each god; each grace amain,
Every joy and virtue speed,
Marching duly in her train,
And fainting Nature at her need
Is made whole again.

'Twas the vintage-day of field and wood,
When magic wine for bards is brewed;
Every tree and stem and chink
Gushed with syrup to the brink.
The air stole into the streets of towns,
Refreshed the wise, reformed the clowns,
And betrayed the fund of joy
To the high-school and medalled boy:
On from hall to chamber ran,
From youth to maid, from boy to man,
To babes, and to old eyes as well.
'Once more,' the old man cried, 'ye clouds,
Airy turrets purple-piled,
Which once my infancy beguiled,
Beguile me with the wonted spell.
I know ye skilful to convoy
The total freight of hope and joy
Into rude and homely nooks,
Shed mocking lustres on shelf of books,
On farmer's byre, on pasture rude,
And stony pathway to the wood.
I care not if the pomps you show

Be what they soothfast appear,
Or if yon realms in sunset glow
Be bubbles of the atmosphere.
And if it be to you allowed
To fool me with a shining cloud,
So only new griefs are consoled
By new delights, as old by old,
Frankly I will be your guest,
Count your change and cheer the best.
The world hath overmuch of pain,—
If Nature give me joy again,
Of such deceit I'll not complain.'

Ah! well I mind the calendar,
Faithful through a thousand years,
Of the painted race of flowers,
Exact to days, exact to hours,
Counted on the spacious dial
Yon broidered zodiac girds.
I know the trusty almanac
Of the punctual coming-back,
On their due days, of the birds.
I marked them yestermorn,
A flock of finches darting
Beneath the crystal arch,
Piping, as they flew, a march,—
Belike the one they used in parting
Last year from yon oak or larch;
Dusky sparrows in a crowd,
Diving, darting northward free,
Suddenly betook them all,
Every one to his hole in the wall,
Or to his niche in the apple-tree.
I greet with joy the choral trains
Fresh from palms and Cuba's canes.

Best gems of Nature's cabinet,
With dews of tropic morning wet,
Beloved of children, bards and Spring,
O birds, your perfect virtues bring,
Your song, your forms, your rhythmic flight,
Your manners for the heart's delight,
Nestle in hedge, or barn, or roof,
Here weave your chamber weather-proof,
Forgive our harms, and condescend
To man, as to a lubber friend,
And, generous, teach his awkward race
Courage and probity and grace!

Poets praise that hidden wine
Hid in milk we drew
At the barrier of Time,
When our life was new.
We had eaten fairy fruit,
We were quick from head to foot,
All the forms we looked on shone
As with diamond dews thereon.
What cared we for costly joys,
The Museum's far-fetched toys?
Gleam of sunshine on the wall
Poured a deeper cheer than all
The revels of the Carnival.
We a pine-grove did prefer
To a marble theatre,
Could with gods on mallows dine,
Nor cared for spices or for wine.
Wreaths of mist and rainbow spanned.
Arch on arch, the grimmest land;
Whittle of a woodland bird
Made the pulses dance,
Note of horn in valleys heard

Filled the region with romance.

None can tell how sweet,
How virtuous, the morning air;
Every accent vibrates well;
Not alone the wood-bird's call,
Or shouting boys that chase their ball,
Pass the height of minstrel skill,
But the ploughman's thoughtless cry,
Lowing oxen, sheep that bleat,
And the joiner's hammer-beat,
Softened are above their will,
Take tones from groves they wandered through
Or flutes which passing angels blew.
All grating discords melt,
No dissonant note is dealt,
And though thy voice be shrill
Like rasping file on steel,
Such is the temper of the air,
Echo waits with art and care,
And will the faults of song repair.

So by remote Superior Lake,
And by resounding Mackinac,
When northern storms the forest shake,
And billows on the long beach break,
The artful Air will separate
Note by note all sounds that grate,
Smothering in her ample breast
All but godlike words,
Reporting to the happy ear
Only purified accords.
Strangely wrought from barking waves,
Soft music daunts the Indian braves, —
Convent-chanting which the child

Hears pealing from the panther's cave
And the impenetrable wild.

Soft on the South-wind sleeps the haze:
So on thy broad mystic van
Lie the opal-colored days,
And waft the miracle to man.
Soothsayer of the eldest gods,
Repairer of what harms betide,
Revealer of the inmost powers
Prometheus proffered, Jove denied;
Disclosing treasures more than true,
Or in what far to-morrow due;
Speaking by the tongues of flowers,
By the ten-tongued laurel speaking,
Singing by the oriole songs,
Heart of bird the man's heart seeking;
Whispering hints of treasure hid
Under Morn's unlifted lid,
Islands looming just beyond
The dim horizon's utmost bound;—
Who can, like thee, our rags upbraid,
Or taunt us with our hope decayed?
Or who like thee persuade,
Making the splendor of the air,
The morn and sparkling dew, a snare?
Or who resent
Thy genius, wiles and blandishment?

There is no orator prevails
To beckon or persuade
Like thee the youth or maid:
Thy birds, thy songs, thy brooks, thy gales,
Thy blooms, thy kinds,
Thy echoes in the wilderness,

Soothe pain, and age, and love's distress,
Fire fainting will, and build heroic minds.

For thou, O Spring! canst renovate
All that high God did first create.
Be still his arm and architect,
Rebuild the ruin, mend defect;
Chemist to vamp old worlds with new,
Coat sea and sky with heavenlier blue,
New tint the plumage of the birds,
And slough decay from grazing herds,
Sweep ruins from the scarped mountain,
Cleanse the torrent at the fountain,
Purge alpine air by towns defiled,
Bring to fair mother fairer child,
Not less renew the heart and brain,
Scatter the sloth, wash out the stain,
Make the aged eye sun-clear,
To parting soul bring grandeur near.
Under gentle types, my Spring
Masks the might of Nature's king,
An energy that searches thorough
From Chaos to the dawning morrow;
Into all our human plight,
The soul's pilgrimage and flight;
In city or in solitude,
Step by step, lifts bad to good,
Without halting, without rest,
Lifting Better up to Best;
Planting seeds of knowledge pure,
Through earth to ripen, through heaven endure.

THE ADIRONDACS

A JOURNAL

DEDICATED TO MY FELLOW TRAVELLERS IN
AUGUST, 1858

Wise and polite,—and if I drew
Their several portraits, you would own
Chaucer had no such worthy crew,
Nor Boccace in Decameron.

We crossed Champlain to Keeseville with our friends,
Thence, in strong country carts, rode up the forks
Of the Ausable stream, intent to reach
The Adirondac lakes. At Martin's Beach
We chose our boats; each man a boat and guide,—
Ten men, ten guides, our company all told.

Next morn, we swept with oars the Saranac,
With skies of benediction, to Round Lake,
Where all the sacred mountains drew around us,
Taháwus, Seaward, MacIntyre, Baldhead,
And other Titans without muse or name.
Pleased with these grand companions, we glide on,
Instead of flowers, crowned with a wreath of hills.
We made our distance wider, boat from boat,
As each would hear the oracle alone.
By the bright morn the gay flotilla slid
Through files of flags that gleamed like bayonets,
Through gold-moth-haunted beds of pickerel-flower,
Through scented banks of lilies white and gold,

Where the deer feeds at night, the teal by day,
On through the Upper Saranac, and up
Père Raquette stream, to a small tortuous pass
Winding through grassy shallows in and out,
Two creeping miles of rushes, pads and sponge,
To Follansbee Water and the Lake of Loons.

Northward the length of Follansbee we rowed,
Under low mountains, whose unbroken ridge
Ponderous with beechen forest sloped the shore.
A pause and council: then, where near the head
Due east a bay makes inward to the land
Between two rocky arms, we climb the bank,
And in the twilight of the forest noon
Wield the first axe these echoes ever heard.
We cut young trees to make our poles and thwarts,
Barked the white spruce to weatherfend the roof,
Then struck a light and kindled the camp-fire.

The wood was sovran with centennial trees, —
Oak, cedar, maple, poplar, beech and fir,
Linden and spruce. In strict society
Three conifers, white, pitch and Norway pine,
Five-leaved, three-leaved and two-leaved, grew thereby,
Our patron pine was fifteen feet in girth,
The maple eight, beneath its shapely tower.

'Welcome!' the wood-god murmured through the leaves, —
'Welcome, though late, unknowing, yet known to me.'
Evening drew on; stars peeped through maple-boughs,
Which o'erhung, like a cloud, our camping fire.
Decayed millennial trunks, like moonlight flecks,
Lit with phosphoric crumbs the forest floor.

Ten scholars, wonted to lie warm and soft
In well-hung chambers daintily bestowed,

Lie here on hemlock-boughs, like Sacs and Sioux,
And greet unanimous the joyful change.
So fast will Nature acclimate her sons,
Though late returning to her pristine ways.
Off soundings, seamen do not suffer cold;
And, in the forest, delicate clerks, unbrowned,
Sleep on the fragrant brush, as on down-beds.
Up with the dawn, they fancied the light air
That circled freshly in their forest dress
Made them to boys again. Happier that they
Slipped off their pack of duties, leagues behind,
At the first mounting of the giant stairs.
No placard on these rocks warned to the polls,
No door-bell heralded a visitor,
No courier waits, no letter came or went,
Nothing was ploughed, or reaped, or bought, or sold;
The frost might glitter, it would blight no crop,
The falling rain will spoil no holiday.
We were made freemen of the forest laws,
All dressed, like Nature, fit for her own ends,
Essaying nothing she cannot perform.

In Adirondac lakes
At morn or noon, the guide rows bareheaded:
Shoes, flannel shirt, and kersey trousers make
His brief toilette: at night, or in the rain,
He dons a surcoat which he doffs at morn:
A paddle in the right hand, or an oar,
And in the left, a gun, his needful arms.
By turns we praised the stature of our guides,
Their rival strength and suppleness, their skill
To row, to swim, to shoot, to build a camp,
To climb a lofty stem, clean without boughs
Full fifty feet, and bring the eaglet down:
Temper to face wolf, bear, or catamount,

And wit to trap or take him in his lair.
Sound, ruddy men, frolic and innocent,
In winter, lumberers; in summer, guides;
Their sinewy arms pull at the oar untired
Three times ten thousand strokes, from morn to eve.

Look to yourselves, ye polished gentlemen!
No city airs or arts pass current here.
Your rank is all reversed; let men or cloth
Bow to the stalwart churls in overalls:
They are the doctors of the wilderness,
And we the low-prized laymen.
In sooth, red flannel is a saucy test
Which few can put on with impunity.
What make you, master, fumbling at the oar?
Will you catch crabs? Truth tries pretension here.
The sallow knows the basket-maker's thumb;
The oar, the guide's. Dare you accept the tasks
He shall impose, to find a spring, trap foxes,
Tell the sun's time, determine the true north,
Or stumbling on through vast self-similar woods
To thread by night the nearest way to camp?

Ask you, how went the hours?
All day we swept the lake, searched every cove,
North from Camp Maple, south to Osprey Bay,
Watching when the loud dogs should drive in deer,
Or whipping its rough surface for a trout;
Or, bathers, diving from the rock at noon;
Challenging Echo by our guns and cries;
Or listening to the laughter of the loon;
Or, in the evening twilight's latest red,
Beholding the procession of the pines;
Or, later yet, beneath a lighted jack,
In the boat's bows, a silent night-hunter

Stealing with paddle to the feeding-grounds
Of the red deer, to aim at a square mist.
Hark to that muffled roar! a tree in the woods
Is fallen: but hush! it has not scared the buck
Who stands astonished at the meteor light,
Then turns to bound away,—is it too late?

Our heroes tried their rifles at a mark,
Six rods, sixteen, twenty, or forty-five;
Sometimes their wits at sally and retort,
With laughter sudden as the crack of rifle;
Or parties scaled the near acclivities
Competing seekers of a rumored lake,
Whose unauthenticated waves we named
Lake Probability,—our carbuncle,
Long sought, not found.

Two Doctors in the camp
Dissected the slain deer, weighed the trout's brain,
Captured the lizard, salamander, shrew,
Crab, mice, snail, dragon-fly, minnow and moth;
Insatiate skill in water or in air
Waved the scoop-net, and nothing came amiss;
The while, one leaden got of alcohol
Gave an impartial tomb to all the kinds.
Not less the ambitious botanist sought plants,
Orchis and gentian, fern and long whip-scirpus,
Rosy polygonum, lake-margin's pride,
Hypnum and hydnum, mushroom, sponge and moss,
Or harebell nodding in the gorge of falls.
Above, the eagle flew, the osprey screamed,
The raven croaked, owls hooted, the woodpecker
Loud hammered, and the heron rose in the swamp.
As water poured through hollows of the hills
To feed this wealth of lakes and rivulets,

So Nature shed all beauty lavishly
From her redundant horn.

Lords of this realm,
Bounded by dawn and sunset, and the day
Rounded by hours where each outdid the last
In miracles of pomp, we must be proud,
As if associates of the sylvan gods.
We seemed the dwellers of the zodiac,
So pure the Alpine element we breathed,
So light, so lofty pictures came and went.
We trode on air, contemned the distant town,
Its timorous ways, big trifles, and we planned
That we should build, hard-by, a spacious lodge
And how we should come hither with our sons,
Hereafter,—willing they, and more adroit.

Hard fare, hard bed and comic misery,—
The midge, the blue-fly and the mosquito
Painted our necks, hands, ankles, with red bands:
But, on the second day, we heed them not,
Nay, we saluted them Auxiliaries,
Whom earlier we had chid with spiteful names.
For who defends our leafy tabernacle
From bold intrusion of the travelling crowd,—
Who but the midge, mosquito and the fly,
Which past endurance sting the tender cit,
But which we learn to scatter with a smudge,
Or baffle by a veil, or slight by scorn?

Our foaming ale we drank from hunters' pans,
Ale, and a sup of wine. Our steward gave
Venison and trout, potatoes, beans, wheat-bread;
All ate like abbots, and, if any missed
Their wonted convenance, cheerly hid the loss
With hunters' appetite and peals of mirth.

And Stillman, our guides' guide, and Commodore,
Crusoe, Crusader, Pius Aeneas, said aloud,
"Chronic dyspepsia never came from eating
Food indigestible":—then murmured some,
Others applauded him who spoke the truth.

Nor doubt but visitings of graver thought
Checked in these souls the turbulent heyday
'Mid all the hints and glories of the home.
For who can tell what sudden privacies
Were sought and found, amid the hue and cry
Of scholars furloughed from their tasks and let
Into this Oreads' fended Paradise,
As chapels in the city's thoroughfares,
Whither gaunt Labor slips to wipe his brow
And meditate a moment on Heaven's rest.
Judge with what sweet surprises Nature spoke
To each apart, lifting her lovely shows
To spiritual lessons pointed home,
And as through dreams in watches of the night,
So through all creatures in their form and ways
Some mystic hint accosts the vigilant,
Not clearly voiced, but waking a new sense
Inviting to new knowledge, one with old.
Hark to that petulant chirp! what ails the warbler?
Mark his capricious ways to draw the eye.
Now soar again. What wilt thou, restless bird,
Seeking in that chaste blue a bluer light,
Thirsting in that pure for a purer sky?

And presently the sky is changed; O world!
What pictures and what harmonies are thine!
The clouds are rich and dark, the air serene,
So like the soul of me, what if 't were me?
A melancholy better than all mirth.

Comes the sweet sadness at the retrospect,
Or at the foresight of obscurer years?
Like yon slow-sailing cloudy promontory
Whereon the purple iris dwells in beauty
Superior to all its gaudy skirts.
And, that no day of life may lack romance,
The spiritual stars rise nightly, shedding down
A private beam into each several heart.
Daily the bending skies solicit man,
The seasons chariot him from this exile,
The rainbow hours bedeck his glowing chair,
The storm-winds urge the heavy weeks along,
Suns haste to set, that so remoter lights
Beckon the wanderer to his vaster home.

With a vermilion pencil mark the day
When of our little fleet three cruising skiffs
Entering Big Tupper, bound for the foaming Falls
Of loud Bog River, suddenly confront
Two of our mates returning with swift oars.
One held a printed journal waving high
Caught from a late-arriving traveller,
Big with great news, and shouted the report
For which the world had waited, now firm fact,
Of the wire-cable laid beneath the sea,
And landed on our coast, and pulsating
With ductile fire. Loud, exulting cries
From boat to boat, and to the echoes round,
Greet the glad miracle. Thought's new-found path
Shall supplement henceforth all trodden ways,
Match God's equator with a zone of art,
And lift man's public action to a height
Worthy the enormous cloud of witnesses,
When linkèd hemispheres attest his deed.
We have few moments in the longest life

Of such delight and wonder as there grew, —
Nor yet unsuited to that solitude:
A burst of joy, as if we told the fact
To ears intelligent; as if gray rock
And cedar grove and cliff and lake should know
This feat of wit, this triumph of mankind;
As if we men were talking in a vein
Of sympathy so large, that ours was theirs,
And a prime end of the most subtle element
Were fairly reached at last. Wake, echoing caves!
Bend nearer, faint day-moon! Yon thundertops,
Let them hear well! 'tis theirs as much as ours.

A spasm throbbing through the pedestals
Of Alp and Andes, isle and continent,
Urging astonished Chaos with a thrill
To be a brain, or serve the brain of man.
The lightning has run masterless too long;
He must to school and learn his verb and noun
And teach his nimbleness to earn his wage,
Spelling with guided tongue man's messages
Shot through the weltering pit of the salt sea.
And yet I marked, even in the manly joy
Of our great-hearted Doctor in his boat
(Perchance I erred), a shade of discontent;
Or was it for mankind a generous shame,
As of a luck not quite legitimate,
Since fortune snatched from wit the lion's part?
Was it a college pique of town and gown,
As one within whose memory it burned
That not academicians, but some lout,
Found ten years since the Californian gold?
And now, again, a hungry company
Of traders, led by corporate sons of trade,
Perversely borrowing from the shop the tools

Of science, not from the philosophers,
Had won the brightest laurel of all time.
'Twas always thus, and will be; hand and head
Are ever rivals: but, though this be swift,
The other slow,—this the Prometheus,
And that the Jove,—yet, howsoever hid,
It was from Jove the other stole his fire,
And, without Jove, the good had never been.
It is not Iroquois or cannibals,
But ever the free race with front sublime,
And these instructed by their wisest too,
Who do the feat, and lift humanity.
Let not him mourn who best entitled was,
Nay, mourn not one: let him exult,
Yea, plant the tree that bears best apples, plant,
And water it with wine, nor watch askance
Whether thy sons or strangers eat the fruit:
Enough that mankind eat and are refreshed.

We flee away from cities, but we bring
The best of cities with us, these learned classifiers,
Men knowing what they seek, armed eyes of experts.
We praise the guide, we praise the forest life:
But will we sacrifice our dear-bought lore
Of books and arts and trained experiment,
Or count the Sioux a match for Agassiz?
O no, not we! Witness the shout that shook
Wild Tupper Lake; witness the mute all-hail
The joyful traveller gives, when on the verge
Of craggy Indian wilderness he hears
From a log cabin stream Beethoven's notes
On the piano, played with master's hand.
'Well done!' he cries; 'the bear is kept at bay,
The lynx, the rattlesnake, the flood, the fire;
All the fierce enemies, ague, hunger, cold,

This thin spruce roof, this clayed log-wall,
This wild plantation will suffice to chase.
Now speed the gay celerities of art,
What in the desert was impossible
Within four walls is possible again, —
Culture and libraries, mysteries of skill,
Traditioned fame of masters, eager strife
Of keen competing youths, joined or alone
To outdo each other and extort applause.
Mind wakes a new-born giant from her sleep.
Twirl the old wheels! Time takes fresh start again,
On for a thousand years of genius more.'

The holidays were fruitful, but must end;
One August evening had a cooler breath;
Into each mind intruding duties crept;
Under the cinders burned the fires of home;
Nay, letters found us in our paradise:
So in the gladness of the new event
We struck our camp and left the happy hills.
The fortunate star that rose on us sank not;
The prodigal sunshine rested on the land,
The rivers gambolled onward to the sea,
And Nature, the inscrutable and mute,
Permitted on her infinite repose
Almost a smile to steal to cheer her sons,
As if one riddle of the Sphinx were guessed.

BRAHMA

If the red slayer think he slays,
Or if the slain think he is slain,
They know not well the subtle ways
I keep, and pass, and turn again.

Far or forgot to me is near;
Shadow and sunlight are the same;
The vanished gods to me appear;
And one to me are shame and fame.

They reckon ill who leave me out;
When me they fly, I am the wings;
I am the doubter and the doubt,
And I the hymn the Brahmin sings.

The strong gods pine for my abode,
And pine in vain the sacred Seven;
But thou, meek lover of the good!
Find me, and turn thy back on heaven.

NEMESIS

Already blushes on thy cheek
The bosom thought which thou must speak;
The bird, how far it haply roam
By cloud or isle, is flying home;
The maiden fears, and fearing runs
Into the charmed snare she shuns;
And every man, in love or pride,
Of his fate is never wide.

Will a woman's fan the ocean smooth?
Or prayers the stony Parcae soothe,
Or coax the thunder from its mark?
Or tapers light the chaos dark?
In spite of Virtue and the Muse,
Nemesis will have her dues,
And all our struggles and our toils
Tighter wind the giant coils.

FATE

Deep in the man sits fast his fate
To mould his fortunes, mean or great:
Unknown to Cromwell as to me
Was Cromwell's measure or degree;
Unknown to him as to his horse,
If he than his groom be better or worse.
He works, plots, fights, in rude affairs,
With squires, lords, kings, his craft compares,
Till late he learned, through doubt and fear,
Broad England harbored not his peer:
Obeying time, the last to own
The Genius from its cloudy throne.
For the prevision is allied
Unto the thing so signified;
Or say, the foresight that awaits
Is the same Genius that creates.

FREEDOM

Once I wished I might rehearse
Freedom's paean in my verse,
That the slave who caught the strain
Should throb until he snapped his chain,
But the Spirit said, 'Not so;
Speak it not, or speak it low;
Name not lightly to be said,
Gift too precious to be prayed,
Passion not to be expressed
But by heaving of the breast:
Yet,—wouldst thou the mountain find
Where this deity is shrined,
Who gives to seas and sunset skies
Their unspent beauty of surprise,
And, when it lists him, waken can
Brute or savage into man;
Or, if in thy heart he shine,
Blends the starry fates with thine,
Draws angels nigh to dwell with thee,
And makes thy thoughts archangels be;
Freedom's secret wilt thou know?—
Counsel not with flesh and blood;
Loiter not for cloak or food;
Right thou feelest, rush to do.'

ODE

SUNG IN THE TOWN HALL, CONCORD, JULY 4, 1857

O tenderly the haughty day
Fills his blue urn with fire;
One morn is in the mighty heaven,
And one in our desire.

The cannon booms from town to town,
Our pulses beat not less,
The joy-bells chime their tidings down,
Which children's voices bless.

For He that flung the broad blue fold
O'er-mantling land and sea,
One third part of the sky unrolled
For the banner of the free.

The men are ripe of Saxon kind
To build an equal state, —
To take the statute from the mind
And make of duty fate.

United States! the ages plead, —
Present and Past in under-song, —
Go put your creed into your deed,
Nor speak with double tongue.

For sea and land don't understand,
Nor skies without a frown
See rights for which the one hand fights
By the other cloven down.

Be just at home; then write your scroll
Of honor o'er the sea,
And bid the broad Atlantic roll,
A ferry of the free.

And henceforth there shall be no chain,
Save underneath the sea
The wires shall murmur through the main
Sweet songs of liberty.

The conscious stars accord above,
The waters wild below,
And under, through the cable wove,
Her fiery errands go.

For He that worketh high and wise.
Nor pauses in his plan,
Will take the sun out of the skies
Ere freedom out of man.

BOSTON HYMN

READ IN MUSIC HALL, JANUARY 1, 1863

The word of the Lord by night
To the watching Pilgrims came,
As they sat by the seaside,
And filled their hearts with flame.

God said, I am tired of kings,
I suffer them no more;
Up to my ear the morning brings
The outrage of the poor.

Think ye I made this ball
A field of havoc and war,
Where tyrants great and tyrants small
Might harry the weak and poor?

My angel,—his name is Freedom,—
Choose him to be your king;
He shall cut pathways east and west
And fend you with his wing.

Lo! I uncover the land
Which I hid of old time in the West,
As the sculptor uncovers the statue
When he has wrought his best;

I show Columbia, of the rocks
Which dip their foot in the seas
And soar to the air-borne flocks
Of clouds and the boreal fleece.

I will divide my goods;

Call in the wretch and slave:
None shall rule but the humble.
And none but Toil shall have.

I will have never a noble,
No lineage counted great;
Fishers and choppers and ploughmen
Shall constitute a state.

Go, cut down trees in the forest
And trim the straightest boughs;
Cut down trees in the forest
And build me a wooden house.

Call the people together,
The young men and the sires,
The digger in the harvest-field,
Hireling and him that hires;

And here in a pine state-house
They shall choose men to rule
In every needful faculty,
In church and state and school.

Lo, now! if these poor men
Can govern the land and sea
And make just laws below the sun,
As planets faithful be.

And ye shall succor men;
'Tis nobleness to serve;
Help them who cannot help again:
Beware from right to swerve.

I break your bonds and masterships,
And I unchain the slave:
Free be his heart and hand henceforth
As wind and wandering wave.

I cause from every creature
His proper good to flow:
As much as he is and doeth,
So much he shall bestow.

But, laying hands on another
To coin his labor and sweat,
He goes in pawn to his victim
For eternal years in debt.

To-day unbind the captive,
So only are ye unbound;
Lift up a people from the dust,
Trump of their rescue, sound!

Pay ransom to the owner
And fill the bag to the brim.
Who is the owner? The slave is owner,
And ever was. Pay him.

O North! give him beauty for rags,
And honor, O South! for his shame;
Nevada! coin thy golden crags
With Freedom's image and name.

Up! and the dusky race
That sat in darkness long, —
Be swift their feet as antelopes.
And as behemoth strong.

Come, East and West and North,
By races, as snow-flakes,
And carry my purpose forth,
Which neither halts nor shakes.

My will fulfilled shall be,
For, in daylight or in dark,
My thunderbolt has eyes to see
His way home to the mark.

VOLUNTARIES

I

Low and mournful be the strain,
Haughty thought be far from me;
Tones of penitence and pain,
Meanings of the tropic sea;
Low and tender in the cell
Where a captive sits in chains.
Crooning ditties treasured well
From his Afric's torrid plains.
Sole estate his sire bequeathed,—
Hapless sire to hapless son,—
Was the wailing song he breathed,
And his chain when life was done.

What his fault, or what his crime?
Or what ill planet crossed his prime?
Heart too soft and will too weak
To front the fate that crouches near,—
Dove beneath the vulture's beak;—
Will song dissuade the thirsty spear?
Dragged from his mother's arms and breast,
Displaced, disfurnished here,
His wistful toil to do his best
Chilled by a ribald jeer.
Great men in the Senate sate,
Sage and hero, side by side,
Building for their sons the State,
Which they shall rule with pride.
They forbore to break the chain

Which bound the dusky tribe,
Checked by the owners' fierce disdain,
Lured by 'Union' as the bribe.
Destiny sat by, and said,
'Pang for pang your seed shall pay,
Hide in false peace your coward head,
I bring round the harvest day.'

II

Freedom all winged expands,
Nor perches in a narrow place;
Her broad van seeks unplanted lands;
She loves a poor and virtuous race.
Clinging to a colder zone
Whose dark sky sheds the snowflake down,
The snowflake is her banner's star,
Her stripes the boreal streamers are.
Long she loved the Northman well;
Now the iron age is done,
She will not refuse to dwell
With the offspring of the Sun;
Foundling of the desert far,
Where palms plume, siroccos blaze,
He roves unhurt the burning ways
In climates of the summer star.
He has avenues to God
Hid from men of Northern brain,
Far beholding, without cloud,
What these with slowest steps attain.
If once the generous chief arrive
To lead him willing to be led,
For freedom he will strike and strive,
And drain his heart till he be dead.

III

In an age of fops and toys,

Wanting wisdom, void of right,
Who shall nerve heroic boys
To hazard all in Freedom's fight,—
Break sharply off their jolly games,
Forsake their comrades gay
And quit proud homes and youthful dames
For famine, toil and fray?
Yet on the nimble air benign
Speed nimbler messages,
That waft the breath of grace divine
To hearts in sloth and ease.
So nigh is grandeur to our dust,
So near is God to man,
When Duty whispers low, *Thou must,*
The youth replies, *I can.*
IV

O, well for the fortunate soul
Which Music's wings infold,
Stealing away the memory
Of sorrows new and old!
Yet happier he whose inward sight,
Stayed on his subtile thought,
Shuts his sense on toys of time,
To vacant bosoms brought.
But best befriended of the God
He who, in evil times,
Warned by an inward voice,
Heeds not the darkness and the dread,
Biding by his rule and choice,
Feeling only the fiery thread
Leading over heroic ground,
Walled with mortal terror round,
To the aim which him allures,
And the sweet heaven his deed secures.

Peril around, all else appalling,
Cannon in front and leaden rain
Him duty through the clarion calling
To the van called not in vain.

Stainless soldier on the walls,
Knowing this,—and knows no more,—
Whoever fights, whoever falls,
Justice conquers evermore,
Justice after as before,—
And he who battles on her side,
God, though he were ten times slain,
Crowns him victor glorified,
Victor over death and pain.
V

Blooms the laurel which belongs
To the valiant chief who fights;
I see the wreath, I hear the songs
Lauding the Eternal Rights,
Victors over daily wrongs:
Awful victors, they misguide
Whom they will destroy,
And their coming triumph hide
In our downfall, or our joy:
They reach no term, they never sleep,
In equal strength through space abide;
Though, feigning dwarfs, they crouch and creep,
The strong they slay, the swift outstride:
Fate's grass grows rank in valley clods,
And rankly on the castled steep,—
Speak it firmly, these are gods,
All are ghosts beside.

LOVE AND THOUGHT

Two well-assorted travellers use
The highway, Eros and the Muse.
From the twins is nothing hidden,
To the pair is nought forbidden;
Hand in hand the comrades go
Every nook of Nature through:
Each for other they were born,
Each can other best adorn;
They know one only mortal grief
Past all balsam or relief;
When, by false companions crossed,
The pilgrims have each other lost.

UNA

Roving, roving, as it seems,
Una lights my clouded dreams;
Still for journeys she is dressed;
We wander far by east and west.

In the homestead, homely thought,
At my work I ramble not;
If from home chance draw me wide,
Half-seen Una sits beside.

In my house and garden-plot,
Though beloved, I miss her not;
But one I seek in foreign places,
One face explore in foreign faces.

At home a deeper thought may light
The inward sky with chrysolite,
And I greet from far the ray,
Aurora of a dearer day.

But if upon the seas I sail,
Or trundle on the glowing rail,
I am but a thought of hers,
Loveliest of travellers.

So the gentle poet's name
To foreign parts is blown by fame,
Seek him in his native town,
He is hidden and unknown.

BOSTON

SICUT PATRIBUS, SIT DEUS NOBIS

The rocky nook with hilltops three
Looked eastward from the farms,
And twice each day the flowing sea
Took Boston in its arms;
The men of yore were stout and poor,
And sailed for bread to every shore.

And where they went on trade intent
They did what freemen can,
Their dauntless ways did all men praise,
The merchant was a man.
The world was made for honest trade, —
To plant and eat be none afraid.

The waves that rocked them on the deep
To them their secret told;
Said the winds that sung the lads to sleep,
'Like us be free and bold!'
The honest waves refused to slaves
The empire of the ocean caves.

Old Europe groans with palaces,
Has lords enough and more; —
We plant and build by foaming seas
A city of the poor; —
For day by day could Boston Bay
Their honest labor overpay.

We grant no dukedoms to the few,

We hold like rights, and shall;—
Equal on Sunday in the pew,
On Monday in the mall,
For what avail the plough or sail,
Or land or life, if freedom fail?

The noble craftsman we promote,
Disown the knave and fool;
Each honest man shall have his vote,
Each child shall have his school.
A union then of honest men,
Or union never more again.

The wild rose and the barberry thorn
Hung out their summer pride,
Where now on heated pavements worn
The feet of millions stride.

Fair rose the planted hills behind
The good town on the bay,
And where the western hills declined
The prairie stretched away.

What care though rival cities soar
Along the stormy coast,
Penn's town, New York and Baltimore,
If Boston knew the most!

They laughed to know the world so wide;
The mountains said, 'Good-day!
We greet you well, you Saxon men,
Up with your towns and stay!'
The world was made for honest trade,—
To plant and eat be none afraid.

'For you,' they said, 'no barriers be,
For you no sluggard rest;

Each street leads downward to the sea,
Or landward to the west.'

O happy town beside the sea,
Whose roads lead everywhere to all;
Than thine no deeper moat can be,
No stouter fence, no steeper wall!

Bad news from George on the English throne;
'You are thriving well,' said he;
'Now by these presents be it known
You shall pay us a tax on tea;
'Tis very small,—no load at all,—
Honor enough that we send the call.

'Not so,' said Boston, 'good my lord,
We pay your governors here
Abundant for their bed and board,
Six thousand pounds a year.
(Your Highness knows our homely word)
Millions for self-government,
But for tribute never a cent.'

The cargo came! and who could blame
If *Indians* seized the tea,
And, chest by chest, let down the same,
Into the laughing sea?
For what avail the plough or sail,
Or land or life, if freedom fail?

The townsmen braved the English king,
Found friendship in the French,
And honor joined the patriot ring
Low on their wooden bench.

O bounteous seas that never fail!
O day remembered yet!
O happy port that spied the sail

Which wafted Lafayette!
Pole-star of light in Europe's night,
That never faltered from the right.

Kings shook with fear, old empires crave
The secret force to find
Which fired the little State to save
The rights of all mankind.

But right is might through all the world;
Province to province faithful clung,
Through good and ill the war-bolt hurled,
Till Freedom cheered and joy-bells rung.

The sea returning day by day
Restores the world-wide mart;
So let each dweller on the Bay
Fold Boston in his heart,
Till these echoes be choked with snows,
Or over the town blue ocean flows.

Let the blood of her hundred thousands
Throb in each manly vein;
And the wits of all her wisest,
Make sunshine in her brain.
For you can teach the lightning speech,
And round the globe your voices reach.

And each shall care for other,
And each to each shall bend,
To the poor a noble brother,
To the good an equal friend.

A blessing through the ages thus
Shield all thy roofs and towers!
GOD WITH THE FATHERS, SO WITH US,
Thou darling town of ours!

LETTERS

Every day brings a ship,
Every ship brings a word;
Well for those who have no fear.
Looking seaward, well assured
That the word the vessel brings
Is the word they wish to hear.

RUBIES

They brought me rubies from the mine,
And held them to the sun;
I said, they are drops of frozen wine
From Eden's vats that run.

I looked again,—I thought them hearts
Of friends to friends unknown;
Tides that should warm each neighboring life
Are locked in sparkling stone.

But fire to thaw that ruddy snow,
To break enchanted ice,
And give love's scarlet tides to flow,—
When shall that sun arise?

MERLIN'S SONG

I

Of Merlin wise I learned a song, —
Sing it low or sing it loud,
It is mightier than the strong,
And punishes the proud.
I sing it to the surging crowd, —
Good men it will calm and cheer,
Bad men it will chain and cage—
In the heart of the music peals a strain
Which only angels hear;
Whether it waken joy or rage
Hushed myriads hark in vain,
Yet they who hear it shed their age,
And take their youth again.

II

Hear what British Merlin sung,
Of keenest eye and truest tongue.
Say not, the chiefs who first arrive
Usurp the seats for which all strive;
The forefathers this land who found
Failed to plant the vantage-ground;
Ever from one who comes to-morrow
Men wait their good and truth to borrow.
But wilt thou measure all thy road,
See thou lift the lightest load.
Who has little, to him who has less, can spare,
And thou, Cyndyllan's son! beware
Ponderous gold and stuffs to bear,

To falter ere thou thy task fulfil, —
Only the light-armed climb the hill.
The richest of all lords is Use,
And ruddy Health the loftiest Muse.
Live in the sunshine, swim the sea,
Drink the wild air's salubrity:
When the star Canope shines in May,
Shepherds are thankful and nations gay.
The music that can deepest reach,
And cure all ill, is cordial speech:
Mask thy wisdom with delight,
Toy with the bow, yet hit the white.
Of all wit's uses, the main one
Is to live well with who has none.

THE TEST

(Musa loquitur.)

I hung my verses in the wind,
Time and tide their faults may find.
All were winnowed through and through,
Five lines lasted sound and true;
Five were smelted in a pot
Than the South more fierce and hot;
These the siroc could not melt,
Fire their fiercer flaming felt,
And the meaning was more white
Than July's meridian light.
Sunshine cannot bleach the snow,
Nor time unmake what poets know.
Have you eyes to find the five
Which five hundred did survive?

SOLUTION

I am the Muse who sung alway
By Jove, at dawn of the first day.
Star-crowned, sole-sitting, long I wrought
To fire the stagnant earth with thought:
On spawning slime my song prevails,
Wolves shed their fangs, and dragons scales;
Flushed in the sky the sweet May-morn,
Earth smiled with flowers, and man was born.
Then Asia yeaned her shepherd race,
And Nile substructs her granite base, —
Tented Tartary, columned Nile, —
And, under vines, on rocky isle,
Or on wind-blown sea-marge bleak,
Forward stepped the perfect Greek:
That wit and joy might find a tongue,
And earth grow civil, HOMER sung.

Flown to Italy from Greece,
I brooded long and held my peace,
For I am wont to sing uncalled,
And in days of evil plight
Unlock doors of new delight;
And sometimes mankind I appalled
With a bitter horoscope,
With spasms of terror for balm of hope.
Then by better thought I lead
Bards to speak what nations need;
So I folded me in fears,

And DANTE searched the triple spheres,
Moulding Nature at his will,
So shaped, so colored, swift or still,
And, sculptor-like, his large design
Etched on Alp and Apennine.

Seethed in mists of Penmanmaur,
Taught by Plinlimmon's Druid power,
England's genius filled all measure
Of heart and soul, of strength and pleasure,
Gave to the mind its emperor,
And life was larger than before:
Nor sequent centuries could hit
Orbit and sum of SHAKSPEARE'S wit.
The men who lived with him became
Poets, for the air was fame.

Far in the North, where polar night
Holds in check the frolic light,
In trance upborne past mortal goal
The Swede EMANUEL leads the soul.
Through snows above, mines underground,
The inks of Erebus he found;
Rehearsed to men the damned wails
On which the seraph music sails.
In spirit-worlds he trod alone,
But walked the earth unmarked, unknown,
The near bystander caught no sound,—
Yet they who listened far aloof
Heard rendings of the skyey roof,
And felt, beneath, the quaking ground;
And his air-sown, unheeded words,
In the next age, are flaming swords.

In newer days of war and trade,
Romance forgot, and faith decayed,

When Science armed and guided war,
And clerks the Janus-gates unbar,
When France, where poet never grew,
Halved and dealt the globe anew,
GOETHE, raised o'er joy and strife,
Drew the firm lines of Fate and Life
And brought Olympian wisdom down
To court and mart, to gown and town.
Stooping, his finger wrote in clay
The open secret of to-day.

So bloom the unfading petals five,
And verses that all verse outlive.

HYMN

SUNG AT THE SECOND CHURCH, AT THE
ORDINATION
OF REV. CHANDLER ROBBINS

We love the venerable house
Our fathers built to God;—
In heaven are kept their grateful vows,
Their dust endears the sod.

Here holy thoughts a light have shed
From many a radiant face,
And prayers of humble virtue made
The perfume of the place.

And anxious hearts have pondered here
The mystery of life,
And prayed the eternal Light to clear
Their doubts, and aid their strife.

From humble tenements around
Came up the pensive train,
And in the church a blessing found
That filled their homes again;

For faith and peace and mighty love
That from the Godhead flow,
Showed them the life of Heaven above
Springs from the life below.

They live with God; their homes are dust;
Yet here their children pray,

And in this fleeting lifetime trust
To find the narrow way.

On him who by the altar stands,
On him thy blessing fall,
Speak through his lips thy pure commands,
Thou heart that lovest all.

NATURE I

Winters know
Easily to shed the snow,
And the untaught Spring is wise
In cowslips and anemonies.
Nature, hating art and pains,
Baulks and baffles plotting brains;
Casualty and Surprise
Are the apples of her eyes;
But she dearly loves the poor,
And, by marvel of her own,
Strikes the loud pretender down.
For Nature listens in the rose
And hearkens in the berry's bell
To help her friends, to plague her foes,
And like wise God she judges well.
Yet doth much her love excel
To the souls that never fell,
To swains that live in happiness
And do well because they please,
Who walk in ways that are unfamed,
And feats achieve before they're named.

NATURE II

She is gamesome and good,
But of mutable mood,—
No dreary repeater now and again,
She will be all things to all men.
She who is old, but nowise feeble,
Pours her power into the people,
Merry and manifold without bar,
Makes and moulds them what they are,
And what they call their city way
Is not their way, but hers,
And what they say they made to-day,
They learned of the oaks and firs.
She spawneth men as mallows fresh,
Hero and maiden, flesh of her flesh;
She drugs her water and her wheat
With the flavors she finds meet,
And gives them what to drink and eat;
And having thus their bread and growth,
They do her bidding, nothing loath.
What's most theirs is not their own,
But borrowed in atoms from iron and stone,
And in their vaunted works of Art
The master-stroke is still her part.

THE ROMANY GIRL

The sun goes down, and with him takes
The coarseness of my poor attire;
The fair moon mounts, and aye the flame
Of Gypsy beauty blazes higher.

Pale Northern girls! you scorn our race;
You captives of your air-tight halls,
Wear out indoors your sickly days,
But leave us the horizon walls.

And if I take you, dames, to task,
And say it frankly without guile,
Then you are Gypsies in a mask,
And I the lady all the while.

If on the heath, below the moon,
I court and play with paler blood,
Me false to mine dare whisper none,—
One sallow horseman knows me good.

Go, keep your cheek's rose from the rain,
For teeth and hair with shopmen deal;
My swarthy tint is in the grain,
The rocks and forest know it real.

The wild air bloweth in our lungs,
The keen stars twinkle in our eyes,
The birds gave us our wily tongues,
The panther in our dances flies.

You doubt we read the stars on high,
Nathless we read your fortunes true;
The stars may hide in the upper sky,
But without glass we fathom you.

DAYS

Daughters of Time, the hypocritic Days,
Muffled and dumb like barefoot dervishes,
And marching single in an endless file,
Bring diadems and fagots in their hands.
To each they offer gifts after his will,
Bread, kingdoms, stars, and sky that holds them all.
I, in my pleached garden, watched the pomp,
Forgot my morning wishes, hastily
Took a few herbs and apples, and the Day
Turned and departed silent. I, too late,
Under her solemn fillet saw the scorn.

MY GARDEN

If I could put my woods in song
And tell what's there enjoyed,
All men would to my gardens throng,
And leave the cities void.

In my plot no tulips blow,—
Snow-loving pines and oaks instead;
And rank the savage maples grow
From Spring's faint flush to Autumn red.

My garden is a forest ledge
Which older forests bound;
The banks slope down to the blue lake-edge,
Then plunge to depths profound.

Here once the Deluge ploughed,
Laid the terraces, one by one;
Ebbing later whence it flowed,
They bleach and dry in the sun.

The sowers made haste to depart,—
The wind and the birds which sowed it;
Not for fame, nor by rules of art,
Planted these, and tempests flowed it.

Waters that wash my garden-side
Play not in Nature's lawful web,
They heed not moon or solar tide,—
Five years elapse from flood to ebb.

Hither hasted, in old time, Jove,

And every god,—none did refuse;
And be sure at last came Love,
And after Love, the Muse.

Keen ears can catch a syllable,
As if one spake to another,
In the hemlocks tall, untamable,
And what the whispering grasses smother.

Aeolian harps in the pine
Ring with the song of the Fates;
Infant Bacchus in the vine,—
Far distant yet his chorus waits.

Canst thou copy in verse one chime
Of the wood-bell's peal and cry,
Write in a book the morning's prime,
Or match with words that tender sky?

Wonderful verse of the gods,
Of one import, of varied tone;
They chant the bliss of their abodes
To man imprisoned in his own.

Ever the words of the gods resound;
But the porches of man's ear
Seldom in this low life's round
Are unsealed that he may hear.

Wandering voices in the air
And murmurs in the wold
Speak what I cannot declare,
Yet cannot all withhold.

When the shadow fell on the lake,
The whirlwind in ripples wrote
Air-bells of fortune that shine and break,
And omens above thought.

But the meanings cleave to the lake,
Cannot be carried in book or urn;
Go thy ways now, come later back,
On waves and hedges still they burn.

These the fates of men forecast,
Of better men than live to-day;
If who can read them comes at last
He will spell in the sculpture, 'Stay.'

THE CHARTIST'S COMPLAINT

Day! hast thou two faces,
Making one place two places?
One, by humble farmer seen,
Chill and wet, unlighted, mean,
Useful only, triste and damp,
Serving for a laborer's lamp?
Have the same mists another side,
To be the appanage of pride,
Gracing the rich man's wood and lake,
His park where amber mornings break,
And treacherously bright to show
His planted isle where roses glow?
O Day! and is your mightiness
A sycophant to smug success?
Will the sweet sky and ocean broad
Be fine accomplices to fraud?
O Sun! I curse thy cruel ray:
Back, back to chaos, harlot Day!

THE TITMOUSE

You shall not be overbold
When you deal with arctic cold,
As late I found my lukewarm blood
Chilled wading in the snow-choked wood.
How should I fight? my foeman fine
Has million arms to one of mine:
East, west, for aid I looked in vain,
East, west, north, south, are his domain.
Miles off, three dangerous miles, is home;
Must borrow his winds who there would come.
Up and away for life! be fleet!—
The frost-king ties my fumbling feet,
Sings in my ears, my hands are stones,
Curdles the blood to the marble bones,
Tugs at the heart-strings, numbs the sense,
And hems in life with narrowing fence.
Well, in this broad bed lie and sleep,—
The punctual stars will vigil keep,—
Embalmed by purifying cold;
The winds shall sing their dead-march old,
The snow is no ignoble shroud,
The moon thy mourner, and the cloud.

Softly,—but this way fate was pointing,
'T was coming fast to such anointing,
When piped a tiny voice hard by,
Gay and polite, a cheerful cry,
Chic-chic-a-dee-de! saucy note

Out of sound heart and merry throat,
As if it said, 'Good day, good sir!
Fine afternoon, old passenger!
Happy to meet you in these places,
Where January brings few faces.'

This poet, though he live apart,
Moved by his hospitable heart,
Sped, when I passed his sylvan fort,
To do the honors of his court,
As fits a feathered lord of land;
Flew near, with soft wing grazed my hand,
Hopped on the bough, then, darting low,
Prints his small impress on the snow,
Shows feats of his gymnastic play,
Head downward, clinging to the spray.

Here was this atom in full breath,
Hurling defiance at vast death;
This scrap of valor just for play
Fronts the north-wind in waistcoat gray,
As if to shame my weak behavior;
I greeted loud my little savior,
'You pet! what dost here? and what for?
In these woods, thy small Labrador,
At this pinch, wee San Salvador!
What fire burns in that little chest
So frolic, stout and self-possest?
Henceforth I wear no stripe but thine;
Ashes and jet all hues outshine.
Why are not diamonds black and gray,
To ape thy dare-devil array?
And I affirm, the spacious North
Exists to draw thy virtue forth.
I think no virtue goes with size;

The reason of all cowardice
Is, that men are overgrown,
And, to be valiant, must come down
To the titmouse dimension.'

'T is good will makes intelligence,
And I began to catch the sense
Of my bird's song: 'Live out of doors
In the great woods, on prairie floors.
I dine in the sun; when he sinks in the sea,
I too have a hole in a hollow tree;
And I like less when Summer beats
With stifling beams on these retreats,
Than noontide twilights which snow makes
With tempest of the blinding flakes.
For well the soul, if stout within,
Can arm impregnably the skin;
And polar frost my frame defied,
Made of the air that blows outside.'

With glad remembrance of my debt,
I homeward turn; farewell, my pet!
When here again thy pilgrim comes,
He shall bring store of seeds and crumbs.
Doubt not, so long as earth has bread,
Thou first and foremost shalt be fed;
The Providence that is most large
Takes hearts like thine in special charge,
Helps who for their own need are strong,
And the sky doats on cheerful song.
Henceforth I prize thy wiry chant
O'er all that mass and minster vaunt;
For men mis-hear thy call in Spring,
As 't would accost some frivolous wing,
Crying out of the hazel copse, *Phe-be!*

And, in winter, *Chic-a-dee-dee!*
I think old Caesar must have heard
In northern Gaul my dauntless bird,
And, echoed in some frosty wold,
Borrowed thy battle-numbers bold.
And I will write our annals new,
And thank thee for a better clew,
I, who dreamed not when I came here
To find the antidote of fear,
Now hear thee say in Roman key,
Paean! Veni, vidi, vici.

THE HARP

One musician is sure,
His wisdom will not fail,
He has not tasted wine impure,
Nor bent to passion frail.
Age cannot cloud his memory,
Nor grief untune his voice,
Ranging down the ruled scale
From tone of joy to inward wail,
Tempering the pitch of all
In his windy cave.
He all the fables knows,
And in their causes tells,—
Knows Nature's rarest moods,
Ever on her secret broods.
The Muse of men is coy,
Oft courted will not come;
In palaces and market squares
Entreated, she is dumb;
But my minstrel knows and tells
The counsel of the gods,
Knows of Holy Book the spells,
Knows the law of Night and Day,
And the heart of girl and boy,
The tragic and the gay,
And what is writ on Table Round
Of Arthur and his peers;
What sea and land discoursing say
In sidereal years.

He renders all his lore
In numbers wild as dreams,
Modulating all extremes, —
What the spangled meadow saith
To the children who have faith;
Only to children children sing,
Only to youth will spring be spring.

Who is the Bard thus magnified?
When did he sing? and where abide?

Chief of song where poets feast
Is the wind-harp which thou seest
In the casement at my side.

Aeolian harp,
How strangely wise thy strain!
Gay for youth, gay for youth,
(Sweet is art, but sweeter truth,)
In the hall at summer eve
Fate and Beauty skilled to weave.
From the eager opening strings
Rung loud and bold the song.
Who but loved the wind-harp's note?
How should not the poet doat
On its mystic tongue,
With its primeval memory,
Reporting what old minstrels told
Of Merlin locked the harp within, —
Merlin paying the pain of sin,
Pent in a dungeon made of air, —
And some attain his voice to hear,
Words of pain and cries of fear,
But pillowed all on melody,
As fits the griefs of bards to be.
And what if that all-echoing shell,

Which thus the buried Past can tell,
Should rive the Future, and reveal
What his dread folds would fain conceal?
It shares the secret of the earth,
And of the kinds that owe her birth.
Speaks not of self that mystic tone,
But of the Overgods alone:
It trembles to the cosmic breath, —
As it heareth, so it saith;
Obeying meek the primal Cause,
It is the tongue of mundane laws.
And this, at least, I dare affirm,
Since genius too has bound and term,
There is no bard in all the choir,
Not Homer's self, the poet sire,
Wise Milton's odes of pensive pleasure,
Or Shakspeare, whom no mind can measure,
Nor Collins' verse of tender pain,
Nor Byron's clarion of disdain,
Scott, the delight of generous boys,
Or Wordsworth, Pan's recording voice, —
Not one of all can put in verse,
Or to this presence could rehearse
The sights and voices ravishing
The boy knew on the hills in spring,
When pacing through the oaks he heard
Sharp queries of the sentry-bird,
The heavy grouse's sudden whir,
The rattle of the kingfisher;
Saw bonfires of the harlot flies
In the lowland, when day dies;
Or marked, benighted and forlorn,
The first far signal-fire of morn.
These syllables that Nature spoke,

And the thoughts that in him woke,
Can adequately utter none
Save to his ear the wind-harp lone.
Therein I hear the Parcae reel
The threads of man at their humming wheel,
The threads of life and power and pain,
So sweet and mournful falls the strain.
And best can teach its Delphian chord
How Nature to the soul is moored,
If once again that silent string,
As erst it wont, would thrill and ring.

Not long ago at eventide,
It seemed, so listening, at my side
A window rose, and, to say sooth,
I looked forth on the fields of youth:
I saw fair boys bestriding steeds,
I knew their forms in fancy weeds,
Long, long concealed by sundering fates,
Mates of my youth,—yet not my mates,
Stronger and bolder far than I,
With grace, with genius, well attired,
And then as now from far admired,
Followed with love
They knew not of,
With passion cold and shy.
O joy, for what recoveries rare!
Renewed, I breathe Elysian air,
See youth's glad mates in earliest bloom,—
Break not my dream, obtrusive tomb!
Or teach thou, Spring! the grand recoil
Of life resurgent from the soil
Wherein was dropped the mortal spoil.

SEASHORE

I heard or seemed to hear the chiding Sea
Say, Pilgrim, why so late and slow to come?
Am I not always here, thy summer home?
Is not my voice thy music, morn and eve?
My breath thy healthful climate in the heats,
My touch thy antidote, my bay thy bath?
Was ever building like my terraces?
Was ever couch magnificent as mine?
Lie on the warm rock-ledges, and there learn
A little hut suffices like a town.
I make your sculptured architecture vain,
Vain beside mine. I drive my wedges home,
And carve the coastwise mountain into caves.
Lo! here is Rome and Nineveh and Thebes,
Karnak and Pyramid and Giant's Stairs
Half piled or prostrate; and my newest slab
Older than all thy race.

Behold the Sea,
The opaline, the plentiful and strong,
Yet beautiful as is the rose in June,
Fresh as the trickling rainbow of July;
Sea full of food, the nourisher of kinds,
Purger of earth, and medicine of men;
Creating a sweet climate by my breath,
Washing out harms and griefs from memory,
And, in my mathematic ebb and flow,
Giving a hint of that which changes not.

Rich are the sea-gods:—who gives gifts but they?
They grope the sea for pearls, but more than pearls:
They pluck Force thence, and give it to the wise.
For every wave is wealth to Daedalus,
Wealth to the cunning artist who can work
This matchless strength. Where shall he find, O waves!
A load your Atlas shoulders cannot lift?

I with my hammer pounding evermore
The rocky coast, smite Andes into dust,
Strewing my bed, and, in another age,
Rebuild a continent of better men.
Then I unbar the doors: my paths lead out
The exodus of nations: I disperse
Men to all shores that front the hoary main.

I too have arts and sorceries;
Illusion dwells forever with the wave.
I know what spells are laid. Leave me to deal
With credulous and imaginative man;
For, though he scoop my water in his palm,
A few rods off he deems it gems and clouds.
Planting strange fruits and sunshine on the shore,
I make some coast alluring, some lone isle,
To distant men, who must go there, or die.

SONG OF NATURE

Mine are the night and morning,
The pits of air, the gulf of space,
The sportive sun, the gibbous moon,
The innumerable days.

I hide in the solar glory,
I am dumb in the pealing song,
I rest on the pitch of the torrent,
In slumber I am strong.

No numbers have counted my tallies,
No tribes my house can fill,
I sit by the shining Fount of Life
And pour the deluge still;

And ever by delicate powers
Gathering along the centuries
From race on race the rarest flowers,
My wreath shall nothing miss.

And many a thousand summers
My gardens ripened well,
And light from meliorating stars
With firmer glory fell.

I wrote the past in characters
Of rock and fire the scroll,
The building in the coral sea,
The planting of the coal.

And thefts from satellites and rings
And broken stars I drew,
And out of spent and aged things
I formed the world anew;

What time the gods kept carnival,
Tricked out in star and flower,
And in cramp elf and saurian forms
They swathed their too much power.

Time and Thought were my surveyors,
They laid their courses well,
They boiled the sea, and piled the layers
Of granite, marl and shell.

But he, the man-child glorious,—
Where tarries he the while?
The rainbow shines his harbinger,
The sunset gleams his smile.

My boreal lights leap upward,
Forthright my planets roll,
And still the man-child is not born,
The summit of the whole.

Must time and tide forever run?
Will never my winds go sleep in the west?
Will never my wheels which whirl the sun
And satellites have rest?

Too much of donning and doffing,
Too slow the rainbow fades,
I weary of my robe of snow,
My leaves and my cascades;

I tire of globes and races,
Too long the game is played;
What without him is summer's pomp,
Or winter's frozen shade?

I travail in pain for him,
My creatures travail and wait;
His couriers come by squadrons,
He comes not to the gate.

Twice I have moulded an image,
And thrice outstretched my hand,
Made one of day and one of night
And one of the salt sea-sand.

One in a Judaean manger,
And one by Avon stream,
One over against the mouths of Nile,
And one in the Academe.

I moulded kings and saviors,
And bards o'er kings to rule;—
But fell the starry influence short,
The cup was never full.

Yet whirl the glowing wheels once more,
And mix the bowl again;
Seethe, Fate! the ancient elements,
Heat, cold, wet, dry, and peace, and pain.

Let war and trade and creeds and song
Blend, ripen race on race,
The sunburnt world a man shall breed
Of all the zones and countless days.

No ray is dimmed, no atom worn,
My oldest force is good as new,
And the fresh rose on yonder thorn
Gives back the bending heavens in dew.

TWO RIVERS

Thy summer voice, Musketaquit,
Repeats the music of the rain;
But sweeter rivers pulsing flit
Through thee, as thou through Concord Plain.

Thou in thy narrow banks art pent:
The stream I love unbounded goes
Through flood and sea and firmament;
Through light, through life, it forward flows.

I see the inundation sweet,
I hear the spending of the stream
Through years, through men, through Nature fleet,
Through love and thought, through power and dream.

Musketaquit, a goblin strong,
Of shard and flint makes jewels gay;
They lose their grief who hear his song,
And where he winds is the day of day.

So forth and brighter fares my stream,—
Who drink it shall not thirst again;
No darkness stains its equal gleam.
And ages drop in it like rain.

WALDEINSAMKEIT

I do not count the hours I spend
In wandering by the sea;
The forest is my loyal friend,
Like God it useth me.

In plains that room for shadows make
Of skirting hills to lie,
Bound in by streams which give and take
Their colors from the sky;

Or on the mountain-crest sublime,
Or down the oaken glade,
O what have I to do with time?
For this the day was made.

Cities of mortals woe-begone
Fantastic care derides,
But in the serious landscape lone
Stern benefit abides.

Sheen will tarnish, honey cloy,
And merry is only a mask of sad,
But, sober on a fund of joy,
The woods at heart are glad.

There the great Planter plants
Of fruitful worlds the grain,
And with a million spells enchants
The souls that walk in pain.

Still on the seeds of all he made

The rose of beauty burns;
Through times that wear and forms that fade,
Immortal youth returns.

The black ducks mounting from the lake,
The pigeon in the pines,
The bittern's boom, a desert make
Which no false art refines.

Down in yon watery nook,
Where bearded mists divide,
The gray old gods whom Chaos knew,
The sires of Nature, hide.

Aloft, in secret veins of air,
Blows the sweet breath of song,
O, few to scale those uplands dare,
Though they to all belong!

See thou bring not to field or stone
The fancies found in books;
Leave authors' eyes, and fetch your own,
To brave the landscape's looks.

Oblivion here thy wisdom is,
Thy thrift, the sleep of cares;
For a proud idleness like this
Crowns all thy mean affairs.

TERMINUS

It is time to be old,
To take in sail:—
The god of bounds,
Who sets to seas a shore,
Came to me in his fatal rounds,
And said: 'No more!
No farther shoot
Thy broad ambitious branches, and thy root.
Fancy departs: no more invent;
Contract thy firmament
To compass of a tent.
There's not enough for this and that,
Make thy option which of two;
Economize the failing river,
Not the less revere the Giver,
Leave the many and hold the few.
Timely wise accept the terms,
Soften the fall with wary foot;
A little while
Still plan and smile,
And,—fault of novel germs,—
Mature the unfallen fruit.
Curse, if thou wilt, thy sires,
Bad husbands of their fires,
Who, when they gave thee breath,
Failed to bequeath
The needful sinew stark as once,
The Baresark marrow to thy bones,

But left a legacy of ebbing veins,
Inconstant heat and nerveless reins, —
Amid the Muses, left thee deaf and dumb,
Amid the gladiators, halt and numb.'

As the bird trims her to the gale,
I trim myself to the storm of time,
I man the rudder, reef the sail,
Obey the voice at eve obeyed at prime:
'Lowly faithful, banish fear,
Right onward drive unharmed;
The port, well worth the cruise, is near,
And every wave is charmed.'

THE NUN'S ASPIRATION

The yesterday doth never smile,
The day goes drudging through the while,
Yet, in the name of Godhead, I
The morrow front, and can defy;
Though I am weak, yet God, when prayed,
Cannot withhold his conquering aid.
Ah me! it was my childhood's thought,
If He should make my web a blot
On life's fair picture of delight,
My heart's content would find it right.
But O, these waves and leaves,—
When happy stoic Nature grieves,
No human speech so beautiful
As their murmurs mine to lull.
On this altar God hath built
I lay my vanity and guilt;
Nor me can Hope or Passion urge
Hearing as now the lofty dirge
Which blasts of Northern mountains hymn,
Nature's funeral high and dim,—
Sable pageantry of clouds,
Mourning summer laid in shrouds.
Many a day shall dawn and die,
Many an angel wander by,
And passing, light my sunken turf
Moist perhaps by ocean surf,
Forgotten amid splendid tombs,
Yet wreathed and hid by summer blooms.

On earth I dream;—I die to be:
Time, shake not thy bald head at me.
I challenge thee to hurry past
Or for my turn to fly too fast.
Think me not numbed or halt with age,
Or cares that earth to earth engage,
Caught with love's cord of twisted beams,
Or mired by climate's gross extremes.
I tire of shams, I rush to be:
I pass with yonder comet free,—
Pass with the comet into space
Which mocks thy aeons to embrace;
Aeons which tardily unfold
Realm beyond realm,—extent untold;
No early morn, no evening late,—
Realms self-upheld, disdaining Fate,
Whose shining sons, too great for fame,
Never heard thy weary name;
Nor lives the tragic bard to say
How drear the part I held in one,
How lame the other limped away.

APRIL

The April winds are magical
And thrill our tuneful frames;
The garden walks are passional
To bachelors and dames.
The hedge is gemmed with diamonds,
The air with Cupids full,
The cobweb clues of Rosamond
Guide lovers to the pool.
Each dimple in the water,
Each leaf that shades the rock
Can cozen, pique and flatter,
Can parley and provoke.
Goodfellow, Puck and goblins,
Know more than any book.
Down with your doleful problems,
And court the sunny brook.
The south-winds are quick-witted,
The schools are sad and slow,
The masters quite omitted
The lore we care to know.

MAIDEN SPEECH OF THE AEOLIAN HARP

Soft and softlier hold me, friends!
Thanks if your genial care
Unbind and give me to the air.
Keep your lips or finger-tips
For flute or spinet's dancing chips;
I await a tenderer touch,
I ask more or not so much:
Give me to the atmosphere,—
Where is the wind, my brother,—where?
Lift the sash, lay me within,
Lend me your ears, and I begin.
For gentle harp to gentle hearts
The secret of the world imparts;
And not to-day and not to-morrow
Can drain its wealth of hope and sorrow;
But day by day, to loving ear
Unlocks new sense and loftier cheer.
I've come to live with you, sweet friends,
This home my minstrel-journeyings ends.
Many and subtle are my lays,
The latest better than the first,
For I can mend the happiest days
And charm the anguish of the worst.

CUPIDO

The solid, solid universe
Is pervious to Love;
With bandaged eyes he never errs,
Around, below, above.
His blinding light
He flingeth white
On God's and Satan's brood,
And reconciles
By mystic wiles
The evil and the good.

THE PAST

The debt is paid,
The verdict said,
The Furies laid,
The plague is stayed.
All fortunes made;
Turn the key and bolt the door,
Sweet is death forevermore.
Nor haughty hope, nor swart chagrin,
Nor murdering hate, can enter in.
All is now secure and fast;
Not the gods can shake the Past;
Flies-to the adamantine door
Bolted down forevermore.
None can reënter there,—
No thief so politic,
No Satan with a royal trick
Steal in by window, chink, or hole,
To bind or unbind, add what lacked,
Insert a leaf, or forge a name,
New-face or finish what is packed,
Alter or mend eternal Fact.

THE LAST FAREWELL

LINES WRITTEN BY THE AUTHOR'S BROTHER,
EDWARD BLISS EMERSON, WHILST SAILING OUT
OF BOSTON HARBOR, BOUND FOR THE ISLAND OF
PORTO RICO, IN 1832

Farewell, ye lofty spires
That cheered the holy light!
Farewell, domestic fires
That broke the gloom of night!
Too soon those spires are lost,
Too fast we leave the bay,
Too soon by ocean tost
From hearth and home away,
Far away, far away.

Farewell the busy town,
The wealthy and the wise,
Kind smile and honest frown
From bright, familiar eyes.
All these are fading now;
Our brig hastes on her way,
Her unremembering prow
Is leaping o'er the sea,
Far away, far away.

Farewell, my mother fond,
Too kind, too good to me;
Nor pearl nor diamond
Would pay my debt to thee.

But even thy kiss denies
Upon my cheek to stay;
The winged vessel flies,
And billows round her play,
Far away, far away.

Farewell, my brothers true,
My betters, yet my peers;
How desert without you
My few and evil years!
But though aye one in heart,
Together sad or gay,
Rude ocean doth us part;
We separate to-day,
Far away, far away.

Farewell, thou fairest one,
Unplighted yet to me,
Uncertain of thine own
I gave my heart to thee.
That untold early love
I leave untold to-day,
My lips in whisper move
Farewell to ...!
Far away, far away.

Farewell I breathe again
To dim New England's shore,
My heart shall beat not when
I pant for thee no more.
In yon green palmy isle,
Beneath the tropic ray,
I murmur never while
For thee and thine I pray;
Far away, far away.

IN MEMORIAM E.B.E.

I mourn upon this battle-field,
But not for those who perished here.
Behold the river-bank
Whither the angry farmers came,
In sloven dress and broken rank,
Nor thought of fame.
Their deed of blood
All mankind praise;
Even the serene Reason says,
It was well done.
The wise and simple have one glance
To greet yon stern head-stone,
Which more of pride than pity gave
To mark the Briton's friendless grave.
Yet it is a stately tomb;
The grand return
Of eve and morn,
The year's fresh bloom,
The silver cloud,
Might grace the dust that is most proud.

Yet not of these I muse
In this ancestral place,
But of a kindred face
That never joy or hope shall here diffuse.

Ah, brother of the brief but blazing star!
What hast thou to do with these
Haunting this bank's historic trees?

Thou born for noblest life,
For action's field, for victor's car,
Thou living champion of the right?
To these their penalty belonged:
I grudge not these their bed of death,
But thine to thee, who never wronged
The poorest that drew breath.

All inborn power that could
Consist with homage to the good
Flamed from his martial eye;
He who seemed a soldier born,
He should have the helmet worn,
All friends to fend, all foes defy,
Fronting foes of God and man,
Frowning down the evil-doer,
Battling for the weak and poor.
His from youth the leader's look
Gave the law which others took,
And never poor beseeching glance
Shamed that sculptured countenance.

There is no record left on earth,
Save in tablets of the heart,
Of the rich inherent worth,
Of the grace that on him shone,
Of eloquent lips, of joyful wit:
He could not frame a word unfit,
An act unworthy to be done;
Honor prompted every glance,
Honor came and sat beside him,
In lowly cot or painful road,
And evermore the cruel god
Cried "Onward!" and the palm-crown showed,
Born for success he seemed,

With grace to win, with heart to hold,
With shining gifts that took all eyes,
With budding power in college-halls,
As pledged in coming days to forge
Weapons to guard the State, or scourge
Tyrants despite their guards or walls.
On his young promise Beauty smiled,
Drew his free homage unbeguiled,
And prosperous Age held out his hand,
And richly his large future planned,
And troops of friends enjoyed the tide,—
All, all was given, and only health denied.

I see him with superior smile
Hunted by Sorrow's grisly train
In lands remote, in toil and pain,
With angel patience labor on,
With the high port he wore erewhile,
When, foremost of the youthful band,
The prizes in all lists he won;
Nor bate one jot of heart or hope,
And, least of all, the loyal tie
Which holds to home 'neath every sky,
The joy and pride the pilgrim feels
In hearts which round the hearth at home
Keep pulse for pulse with those who roam.

What generous beliefs console
The brave whom Fate denies the goal!
If others reach it, is content;
To Heaven's high will his will is bent.
Firm on his heart relied,
What lot soe'er betide,
Work of his hand
He nor repents nor grieves,

Pleads for itself the fact,
As unrepenting Nature leaves
Her every act.

Fell the bolt on the branching oak;
The rainbow of his hope was broke;
No craven cry, no secret tear, —
He told no pang, he knew no fear;
Its peace sublime his aspect kept,
His purpose woke, his features slept;
And yet between the spasms of pain
His genius beamed with joy again.

O'er thy rich dust the endless smile
Of Nature in thy Spanish isle
Hints never loss or cruel break
And sacrifice for love's dear sake,
Nor mourn the unalterable Days
That Genius goes and Folly stays.
What matters how, or from what ground,
The freed soul its Creator found?
Alike thy memory embalms
That orange-grove, that isle of palms,
And these loved banks, whose oak-bough bold
Root in the blood of heroes old.

III
ELEMENTS AND MOTTOES

EXPERIENCE

The lords of life, the lords of life,—
I saw them pass
In their own guise,
Like and unlike,
Portly and grim,—
Use and Surprise,
Surface and Dream,
Succession swift and spectral Wrong,
Temperament without a tongue,
And the inventor of the game
Omnipresent without name;—
Some to see, some to be guessed,
They marched from east to west:
Little man, least of all,
Among the legs of his guardians tall,
Walked about with puzzled look.
Him by the hand dear Nature took,
Dearest Nature, strong and kind,
Whispered, 'Darling, never mind!
To-morrow they will wear another face,
The founder thou; these are thy race!'

COMPENSATION

The wings of Time are black and white,
Pied with morning and with night.
Mountain tall and ocean deep
Trembling balance duly keep.
In changing moon and tidal wave
Glows the feud of Want and Have.
Gauge of more and less through space,
Electric star or pencil plays,
The lonely Earth amid the balls
That hurry through the eternal halls,
A makeweight flying to the void,
Supplemental asteroid,
Or compensatory spark,
Shoots across the neutral Dark.

Man's the elm, and Wealth the vine;
Stanch and strong the tendrils twine:
Though the frail ringlets thee deceive,
None from its stock that vine can reave.
Fear not, then, thou child infirm,
There's no god dare wrong a worm;
Laurel crowns cleave to deserts,
And power to him who power exerts.
Hast not thy share? On winged feet,
Lo it rushes thee to meet;
And all that Nature made thy own,
Floating in air or pent in stone,
Will rive the hills and swim the sea,
And, like thy shadow, follow thee.

POLITICS

Gold and iron are good
To buy iron and gold;
All earth's fleece and food
For their like are sold.
Boded Merlin wise,
Proved Napoleon great,
Nor kind nor coinage buys
Aught above its rate.
Fear, Craft and Avarice
Cannot rear a State.
Out of dust to build
What is more than dust,
Walls Amphion piled
Phoebus stablish must.
When the Muses nine
With the Virtues meet,
Find to their design
An Atlantic seat,
By green orchard boughs
Fended from the heat,
here the statesman ploughs
Furrow for the wheat, —
When the Church is social worth,
When the state-house is the hearth,
Then the perfect State is come,
The republican at home.

HEROISM

Ruby wine is drunk by knaves,
Sugar spends to fatten slaves,
Rose and vine-leaf deck buffoons;
Thunder-clouds are Jove's festoons,
Drooping oft in wreaths of dread,
Lightning-knotted round his head;
The hero is not fed on sweets,
Daily his own heart he eats;
Chambers of the great are jails,
And head-winds right for royal sails.

CHARACTER

The sun set, but set not his hope:
Stars rose; his faith was earlier up:
Fixed on the enormous galaxy,
Deeper and older seemed his eye;
And matched his sufferance sublime
The taciturnity of time.
He spoke, and words more soft than rain
Brought the Age of Gold again:
His action won such reverence sweet
As hid all measure of the feat.

CULTURE

Can rules or tutors educate
The semigod whom we await?
He must be musical,
Tremulous, impressional,
Alive to gentle influence
Of landscape and of sky,
And tender to the spirit-touch
Of man's or maiden's eye:
But, to his native centre fast,
Shall into Future fuse the Past,
And the world's flowing fates in his own mould recast.

FRIENDSHIP

A ruddy drop of manly blood
The surging sea outweighs,
The world uncertain comes and goes;
The lover rooted stays.
I fancied he was fled, —
And, after many a year,
Glowed unexhausted kindliness,
Like daily sunrise there.
My careful heart was free again,
O friend, my bosom said,
Through thee alone the sky is arched,
Through thee the rose is red;
All things through thee take nobler form,
And look beyond the earth,
The mill-round of our fate appears
A sun-path in thy worth.
Me too thy nobleness has taught
To master my despair;
The fountains of my hidden life
Are through thy friendship fair.

SPIRITUAL LAWS

The living Heaven thy prayers respect,
House at once and architect,
Quarrying man's rejected hours,
Builds therewith eternal towers;
Sole and self-commanded works,
Fears not undermining days,
Grows by decays,
And, by the famous might that lurks
In reaction and recoil,
Makes flame to freeze and ice to boil;
Forging, through swart arms of Offence,
The silver seat of Innocence.

BEAUTY

Was never form and never face
So sweet to SEYD as only grace
Which did not slumber like a stone,
But hovered gleaming and was gone.
Beauty chased he everywhere,
In flame, in storm, in clouds of air.
He smote the lake to feed his eye
With the beryl beam of the broken wave;
He flung in pebbles well to hear
The moment's music which they gave.
Oft pealed for him a lofty tone
From nodding pole and belting zone.
He heard a voice none else could hear
From centred and from errant sphere.
The quaking earth did quake in rhyme,
Seas ebbed and flowed in epic chime.
In dens of passion, and pits of woe,
He saw strong Eros struggling through,
To sun the dark and solve the curse,
And beam to the bounds of the universe.
While thus to love he gave his days
In loyal worship, scorning praise,
How spread their lures for him in vain
Thieving Ambition and paltering Gain!
He thought it happier to be dead,
To die for Beauty, than live for bread.

MANNERS

Grace, Beauty and Caprice
Build this golden portal;
Graceful women, chosen men,
Dazzle every mortal.
Their sweet and lofty countenance
His enchanted food;
He need not go to them, their forms
Beset his solitude.
He looketh seldom in their face,
His eyes explore the ground,—
The green grass is a looking-glass
Whereon their traits are found.
Little and less he says to them,
So dances his heart in his breast;
Their tranquil mien bereaveth him
Of wit, of words, of rest.
Too weak to win, too fond to shun
The tyrants of his doom,
The much deceived Endymion
Slips behind a tomb.

ART

Give to barrows, trays and pans
Grace and glimmer of romance;
Bring the moonlight into noon
Hid in gleaming piles of stone;
On the city's paved street
Plant gardens lined with lilacs sweet;
Let spouting fountains cool the air,
Singing in the sun-baked square;
Let statue, picture, park and hall,
Ballad, flag and festival,
The past restore, the day adorn,
And make to-morrow a new morn.
So shall the drudge in dusty frock
Spy behind the city clock
Retinues of airy kings,
Skirts of angels, starry wings,
His fathers shining in bright fables,
His children fed at heavenly tables.
'T is the privilege of Art
Thus to play its cheerful part,
Man on earth to acclimate
And bend the exile to his fate,
And, moulded of one element
With the days and firmament,
Teach him on these as stairs to climb,
And live on even terms with Time;
Whilst upper life the slender rill
Of human sense doth overfill.

UNITY

Space is ample, east and west,
But two cannot go abreast,
Cannot travel in it two:
Yonder masterful cuckoo
Crowds every egg out of the nest,
Quick or dead, except its own;
A spell is laid on sod and stone,
Night and Day were tampered with,
Every quality and pith
Surcharged and sultry with a power
That works its will on age and hour.

WORSHIP

This is he, who, felled by foes,
Sprung harmless up, refreshed by blows:
He to captivity was sold,
But him no prison-bars would hold:
Though they sealed him in a rock,
Mountain chains he can unlock:
Thrown to lions for their meat,
The crouching lion kissed his feet;
Bound to the stake, no flames appalled,
But arched o'er him an honoring vault.
This is he men miscall Fate,
Threading dark ways, arriving late,
But ever coming in time to crown
The truth, and hurl wrong-doers down.
He is the oldest, and best known,
More near than aught thou call'st thy own,
Yet, greeted in another's eyes,
Disconcerts with glad surprise.
This is Jove, who, deaf to prayers,
Floods with blessings unawares.
Draw, if thou canst, the mystic line
Severing rightly his from thine,
Which is human, which divine.

PRUDENCE

Theme no poet gladly sung,
Fair to old and foul to young;
Scorn not thou the love of parts,
And the articles of arts.
Grandeur of the perfect sphere
Thanks the atoms that cohere.

NATURE

I

A subtle chain of countless rings
The next unto the farthest brings;
The eye reads omens where it goes,
And speaks all languages the rose;
And, striving to be man, the worm
Mounts through all the spires of form.

II

The rounded world is fair to see,
Nine times folded in mystery:
Though baffled seers cannot impart
The secret of its laboring heart,
Throb thine with Nature's throbbing breast,
And all is clear from east to west.
Spirit that lurks each form within
Beckons to spirit of its kin;
Self-kindled every atom glows
And hints the future which it owes.

THE INFORMING SPIRIT

I

There is no great and no small
To the Soul that maketh all:
And where it cometh, all things are;
And it cometh everywhere.
II

I am owner of the sphere,
Of the seven stars and the solar year,
Of Caesar's hand, and Plato's brain,
Of Lord Christ's heart, and Shakspeare's strain.

CIRCLES

Nature centres into balls,
And her proud ephemerals,
Fast to surface and outside,
Scan the profile of the sphere;
Knew they what that signified,
A new genesis were here.

INTELLECT

Go, speed the stars of Thought
On to their shining goals;—
The sower scatters broad his seed;
The wheat thou strew'st be souls.

GIFTS

Gifts of one who loved me,—
'T was high time they came;
When he ceased to love me,
Time they stopped for shame.

PROMISE

In countless upward-striving waves
The moon-drawn tide-wave strives;
In thousand far-transplanted grafts
The parent fruit survives;
So, in the new-born millions,
The perfect Adam lives.
Not less are summer mornings dear
To every child they wake,
And each with novel life his sphere
Fills for his proper sake.

CARITAS

In the suburb, in the town,
On the railway, in the square,
Came a beam of goodness down
Doubling daylight everywhere:
Peace now each for malice takes,
Beauty for his sinful weeds,
For the angel Hope aye makes
Him an angel whom she leads.

POWER

His tongue was framed to music,
And his hand was armed with skill;
His face was the mould of beauty,
And his heart the throne of will.

WEALTH

Who shall tell what did befall,
Far away in time, when once,
Over the lifeless ball,
Hung idle stars and suns?
What god the element obeyed?
Wings of what wind the lichen bore,
Wafting the puny seeds of power,
Which, lodged in rock, the rock abrade?
And well the primal pioneer
Knew the strong task to it assigned,
Patient through Heaven's enormous year
To build in matter home for mind.
From air the creeping centuries drew
The matted thicket low and wide,
This must the leaves of ages strew
The granite slab to clothe and hide,
Ere wheat can wave its golden pride.
What smiths, and in what furnace, rolled
(In dizzy aeons dim and mute
The reeling brain can ill compute)
Copper and iron, lead and gold?
What oldest star the fame can save
Of races perishing to pave
The planet with a floor of lime?
Dust is their pyramid and mole:
Who saw what ferns and palms were pressed
Under the tumbling mountain's breast,
In the safe herbal of the coal?

But when the quarried means were piled,
All is waste and worthless, till
Arrives the wise selecting will,
And, out of slime and chaos, Wit
Draws the threads of fair and fit.
Then temples rose, and towns, and marts,
The shop of toil, the hall of arts;
Then flew the sail across the seas
To feed the North from tropic trees;
The storm-wind wove, the torrent span,
Where they were bid, the rivers ran;
New slaves fulfilled the poet's dream,
Galvanic wire, strong-shouldered steam.
Then docks were built, and crops were stored,
And ingots added to the hoard.
But though light-headed man forget,
Remembering Matter pays her debt:
Still, through her motes and masses, draw
Electric thrills and ties of law,
Which bind the strengths of Nature wild
To the conscience of a child.

ILLUSIONS

Flow, flow the waves hated,
Accursed, adored,
The waves of mutation;
No anchorage is.
Sleep is not, death is not;
Who seem to die live.
House you were born in,
Friends of your spring-time,
Old man and young maid,
Day's toil and its guerdon,
They are all vanishing,
Fleeing to fables,
Cannot be moored.
See the stars through them,
Through treacherous marbles.
Know the stars yonder,
The stars everlasting,
Are fugitive also,
And emulate, vaulted,
The lambent heat lightning
And fire-fly's flight.

When thou dost return
On the wave's circulation,
Behold the shimmer,
The wild dissipation,
And, out of endeavor
To change and to flow,

The gas become solid,
And phantoms and nothings
Return to be things,
And endless imbroglio
Is law and the world, —
Then first shalt thou know,
That in the wild turmoil,
Horsed on the Proteus,
Thou ridest to power,
And to endurance.

IV
QUATRAINS AND TRANSLATIONS

QUATRAINS

A.H.

High was her heart, and yet was well inclined,
Her manners made of bounty well refined;
Far capitals and marble courts, her eye still seemed to see,
Minstrels and kings and high-born dames, and of the best
that be.

HUSH!

Every thought is public,
Every nook is wide;
Thy gossips spread each whisper,
And the gods from side to side.

ORATOR

He who has no hands
Perforce must use his tongue;
Foxes are so cunning
Because they are not strong.

ARTIST

Quit the hut, frequent the palace,
Reck not what the people say;
For still, where'er the trees grow biggest,
Huntsmen find the easiest way.

POET

Ever the Poet *from* the land
Steers his bark and trims his sail;
Right out to sea his courses stand,
New worlds to find in pinnace frail.

POET

To clothe the fiery thought
In simple words succeeds,
For still the craft of genius is
To mask a king in weeds.

BOTANIST

Go thou to thy learned task,
I stay with the flowers of Spring:
Do thou of the Ages ask
What me the Hours will bring.

GARDENER

True Brahmin, in the morning meadows wet,
Expound the Vedas of the violet,
Or, hid in vines, peeping through many a loop,
See the plum redden, and the beurré stoop.

FORESTER

He took the color of his vest
From rabbit's coat or grouse's breast;
For, as the wood-kinds lurk and hide,
So walks the woodman, unespied.

NORTHMAN

The gale that wrecked you on the sand,
It helped my rowers to row;
The storm is my best galley hand
And drives me where I go.

FROM ALCUIN

The sea is the road of the bold,
Frontier of the wheat-sown plains,
The pit wherein the streams are rolled
And fountain of the rains.

EXCELSIOR

Over his head were the maple buds,
And over the tree was the moon,
And over the moon were the starry studs
That drop from the angels' shoon.
S.H.

With beams December planets dart
His cold eye truth and conduct scanned,
July was in his sunny heart,
October in his liberal hand.

BORROWING

FROM THE FRENCH

Some of your hurts you have cured,
And the sharpest you still have survived,
But what torments of grief you endured
From evils which never arrived!

NATURE

Boon Nature yields each day a brag which we now first
behold,
And trains us on to slight the new, as if it were the old:
But blest is he, who, playing deep, yet haply asks not why,
Too busied with the crowded hour to fear to live or die.

FATE

Her planted eye to-day controls,
Is in the morrow most at home,
And sternly calls to being souls
That curse her when they come.

HOROSCOPE

Ere he was born, the stars of fate
Plotted to make him rich and great:
When from the womb the babe was loosed,
The gate of gifts behind him closed.

POWER

Cast the bantling on the rocks,
Suckle him with the she-wolf's teat,
Wintered with the hawk and fox,
Power and speed be hands and feet.

CLIMACTERIC

I am not wiser for my age,
Nor skilful by my grief;
Life loiters at the book's first page,—
Ah! could we turn the leaf.

HERI, CRAS, HODIE

Shines the last age, the next with hope is seen,
To-day slinks poorly off unmarked between:
Future or Past no richer secret folds,
O friendless Present! than thy bosom holds.

MEMORY

Night-dreams trace on Memory's wall
Shadows of the thoughts of day,
And thy fortunes, as they fall,
The bias of the will betray.

LOVE

Love on his errand bound to go
Can swim the flood and wade through snow,
Where way is none, 't will creep and wind
And eat through Alps its home to find.

SACRIFICE

Though love repine, and reason chafe,
There came a voice without reply,—
''T is man's perdition to be safe,
When for the truth he ought to die.'

PERICLES

Well and wisely said the Greek,
Be thou faithful, but not fond;
To the altar's foot thy fellow seek,—
The Furies wait beyond.

CASELLA

Test of the poet is knowledge of love,
For Eros is older than Saturn or Jove;
Never was poet, of late or of yore,
Who was not tremulous with love-lore.

SHAKSPEARE

I see all human wits
Are measured but a few;
Unmeasured still my Shakspeare sits,
Lone as the blessed Jew.

HAFIZ

Her passions the shy violet
From Hafiz never hides;
Love-longings of the raptured bird
The bird to him confides.

NATURE IN LEASTS

As sings the pine-tree in the wind,
So sings in the wind a sprig of the pine;
Her strength and soul has laughing France
Shed in each drop of wine.
[Greek: ADAKRYN NEMONTAI AIONA]

'A New commandment,' said the smiling Muse,
'I give my darling son, Thou shalt not preach';—
Luther, Fox, Behmen, Swedenborg, grew pale,
And, on the instant, rosier clouds upbore
Hafiz and Shakspeare with their shining choirs.

TRANSLATIONS

SONNET OF MICHEL ANGELO BUONAROTTI

Never did sculptor's dream unfold
A form which marble doth not hold
In its white block; yet it therein shall find
Only the hand secure and bold
Which still obeys the mind.
So hide in thee, thou heavenly dame,
The ill I shun, the good I claim;
I alas! not well alive,
Miss the aim whereto I strive.
Not love, nor beauty's pride,
Nor Fortune, nor thy coldness, can I chide,
If, whilst within thy heart abide
Both death and pity, my unequal skill
Fails of the life, but draws the death and ill.

THE EXILE

FROM THE PERSIAN OF KERMANI

In Farsistan the violet spreads
Its leaves to the rival sky;
I ask how far is the Tigris flood,
And the vine that grows thereby?

Except the amber morning wind,
Not one salutes me here;
There is no lover in all Bagdat
To offer the exile cheer.

I know that thou, O morning wind!
O'er Kernan's meadow blowest,
And thou, heart-warming nightingale!
My father's orchard knowest.

The merchant hath stuffs of price,
And gems from the sea-washed strand,
And princes offer me grace
To stay in the Syrian land;

But what is gold *for*, but for gifts?
And dark, without love, is the day;
And all that I see in Bagdat
Is the Tigris to float me away.

FROM HAFIZ

I said to heaven that glowed above,
O hide yon sun-filled zone,
Hide all the stars you boast;
For, in the world of love
And estimation true,
The heaped-up harvest of the moon
Is worth one barley-corn at most,
The Pleiads' sheaf but two.

If my darling should depart,
And search the skies for prouder friends,
God forbid my angry heart
In other love should seek amends.

When the blue horizon's hoop
Me a little pinches here,
Instant to my grave I stoop,
And go find thee in the sphere.

EPITAPH

Bethink, poor heart, what bitter kind of jest
Mad Destiny this tender stripling played;
For a warm breast of maiden to his breast,
She laid a slab of marble on his head.

They say, through patience, chalk
Becomes a ruby stone;
Ah, yes! but by the true heart's blood
The chalk is crimson grown.

FRIENDSHIP

Thou foolish Hafiz! Say, do churls
Know the worth of Oman's pearls?
Give the gem which dims the moon
To the noblest, or to none.

Dearest, where thy shadow falls,
Beauty sits and Music calls;
Where thy form and favor come,
All good creatures have their home.

On prince or bride no diamond stone
Half so gracious ever shone,
As the light of enterprise
Beaming from a young man's eyes.

FROM OMAR KHAYYAM

Each spot where tulips prank their state
Has drunk the life-blood of the great;
The violets yon field which stain
Are moles of beauties Time hath slain.

Unbar the door, since thou the Opener art,
Show me the forward way, since thou art guide,
I put no faith in pilot or in chart,
Since they are transient, and thou dost abide.

FROM ALI BEN ABU TALEB

He who has a thousand friends has not a friend to spare,
And he who has one enemy will meet him everywhere.

On two days it steads not to run from thy grave,
The appointed, and the unappointed day;
On the first, neither balm nor physician can save,
Nor thee, on the second, the Universe slay.

FROM IBN JEMIN

Two things thou shalt not long for, if thou love a mind
serene;—

A woman to thy wife, though she were a crowned queen;

And the second, borrowed money,—though the smiling
lender say

That he will not demand the debt until the Judgment Day.

THE FLUTE

FROM HILALI

Hark, what, now loud, now low, the pining flute
complains,

Without tongue, yellow-cheeked, full of winds that wail and
sigh;

Saying, Sweetheart! the old mystery remains,—

If I am I; thou, thou; or thou art I?

TO THE SHAH

FROM HAFIZ

Thy foes to hunt, thy enviers to strike down,
Poises Arcturus aloft morning and evening his spear.

TO THE SHAH

FROM ENWERI

Not in their houses stand the stars,
But o'er the pinnacles of thine!

TO THE SHAH

FROM ENWERI

From thy worth and weight the stars gravitate,
And the equipoise of heaven is thy house's equipoise.

SONG OF SEYD NIMETOLLAH OF KUHISTAN

[Among the religious customs of the dervishes is an
astronomical dance, in which the dervish imitates the
movements of the heavenly bodies, by spinning on his own
axis, whilst at the same time he revolves round the Sheikh
in the centre, representing the sun; and, as he spins, he
sings the Song of Seyd Nimetollah of Kuhistan.]

Spin the ball! I reel, I burn,
Nor head from foot can I discern,
Nor my heart from love of mine,
Nor the wine-cup from the wine.
All my doing, all my leaving,
Reaches not to my perceiving;
Lost in whirling spheres I rove,
And know only that I love.

I am seeker of the stone,
Living gem of Solomon;
From the shore of souls arrived,
In the sea of sense I dived;
But what is land, or what is wave,
To me who only jewels crave?
Love is the air-fed fire intense,
And my heart the frankincense;
As the rich aloes flames, I glow,
Yet the censer cannot know.
I'm all-knowing, yet unknowing;
Stand not, pause not, in my going.

Ask not me, as Muftis can,
To recite the Alcoran;
Well I love the meaning sweet,—
I tread the book beneath my feet.

Lo! the God's love blazes higher,
Till all difference expire.
What are Moslems? what are Giaours?
All are Love's, and all are ours.
I embrace the true believers,
But I reck not of deceivers.
Firm to Heaven my bosom clings,
Heedless of inferior things;
Down on earth there, underfoot,
What men chatter know I not.

V
APPENDIX

THE POET

I

Right upward on the road of fame
With sounding steps the poet came;
Born and nourished in miracles,
His feet were shod with golden bells,
Or where he stepped the soil did peal
As if the dust were glass and steel.
The gallant child where'er he came
Threw to each fact a tuneful name.
The things whereon he cast his eyes
Could not the nations rebaptize,
Nor Time's snows hide the names he set,
Nor last posterity forget.
Yet every scroll whereon he wrote
In latent fire his secret thought,
Fell unregarded to the ground,
Unseen by such as stood around.
The pious wind took it away,
The reverent darkness hid the lay.
Methought like water-haunting birds
Divers or dippers were his words,
And idle clowns beside the mere
At the new vision gape and jeer.
But when the noisy scorn was past,

Emerge the wingèd words in haste.
New-bathed, new-trimmed, on healthy wing,
Right to the heaven they steer and sing.

A Brother of the world, his song
Sounded like a tempest strong
Which tore from oaks their branches broad,
And stars from the ecliptic road.
Times wore he as his clothing-weeds,
He sowed the sun and moon for seeds.
As melts the iceberg in the seas,
As clouds give rain to the eastern breeze,
As snow-banks thaw in April's beam,
The solid kingdoms like a dream
Resist in vain his motive strain,
They totter now and float amain.
For the Muse gave special charge
His learning should be deep and large,
And his training should not scant
The deepest lore of wealth or want:
His flesh should feel, his eyes should read
Every maxim of dreadful Need;
In its fulness he should taste
Life's honeycomb, but not too fast;
Full fed, but not intoxicated;
He should be loved; he should be hated;
A blooming child to children dear,
His heart should palpitate with fear.

And well he loved to quit his home
And, Calmuck, in his wagon roam
To read new landscapes and old skies;—
But oh, to see his solar eyes
Like meteors which chose their way
And rived the dark like a new day!

Not lazy grazing on all they saw,
Each chimney-pot and cottage door,
Farm-gear and village picket-fence,
But, feeding on magnificence,
They bounded to the horizon's edge
And searched with the sun's privilege.
Landward they reached the mountains old
Where pastoral tribes their flocks infold,
Saw rivers run seaward by cities high
And the seas wash the low-hung sky;
Saw the endless rack of the firmament
And the sailing moon where the cloud was rent,
And through man and woman and sea and star
Saw the dance of Nature forward and far,
Through worlds and races and terms and times
Saw musical order and pairing rhymes.

II

The gods talk in the breath of the woods,
They talk in the shaken pine,
And fill the long reach of the old seashore
With dialogue divine;
And the poet who overhears
Some random word they say
Is the fated man of men
Whom the ages must obey:
One who having nectar drank
Into blissful orgies sank;
He takes no mark of night or day,
He cannot go, he cannot stay,
He would, yet would not, counsel keep,
But, like a walker in his sleep
With staring eye that seeth none,
Ridiculously up and down
Seeks how he may fitly tell

The heart-o'erlading miracle.

Not yet, not yet,
Impatient friend, —
A little while attend;
Not yet I sing: but I must wait,
My hand upon the silent string,
Fully until the end.
I see the coming light,
I see the scattered gleams,
Aloft, beneath, on left and right
The stars' own ether beams;
These are but seeds of days,
Not yet a steadfast morn,
An intermittent blaze,
An embryo god unborn.

How all things sparkle,
The dust is alive,
To the birth they arrive:
I snuff the breath of my morning afar,
I see the pale lustres condense to a star:
The fading colors fix,
The vanishing are seen,
And the world that shall be
Twins the world that has been.
I know the appointed hour,
I greet my office well,
Never faster, never slower
Revolves the fatal wheel!
The Fairest enchants me,
The Mighty commands me,
Saying, 'Stand in thy place;
Up and eastward turn thy face;
As mountains for the morning wait,

Coming early, coming late,
So thou attend the enriching Fate
Which none can stay, and none accelerate.
I am neither faint nor weary,
Fill thy will, O faultless heart!
Here from youth to age I tarry,—
Count it flight of bird or dart.
My heart at the heart of things
Heeds no longer lapse of time,
Rushing ages moult their wings,
Bathing in thy day sublime.

The sun set, but set not his hope:—
Stars rose, his faith was earlier up:
Fixed on the enormous galaxy,
Deeper and older seemed his eye,
And matched his sufferance sublime
The taciturnity of Time.

Beside his hut and shading oak,
Thus to himself the poet spoke,
'I have supped to-night with gods,
I will not go under a wooden roof:
As I walked among the hills
In the love which Nature fills,
The great stars did not shine aloof,
They hurried down from their deep abodes
And hemmed me in their glittering troop.

'Divine Inviters! I accept
The courtesy ye have shown and kept
From ancient ages for the bard,
To modulate
With finer fate
A fortune harsh and hard.
With aim like yours

I watch your course,
Who never break your lawful dance
By error or intemperance.
O birds of ether without wings!
O heavenly ships without a sail!
O fire of fire! O best of things!
O mariners who never fail!
Sail swiftly through your amber vault,
An animated law, a presence to exalt.'

Ah, happy if a sun or star
Could chain the wheel of Fortune's car,
And give to hold an even state,
Neither dejected nor elate,
That haply man upraised might keep
The height of Fancy's far-eyed steep.
In vain: the stars are glowing wheels,
Giddy with motion Nature reels,
Sun, moon, man, undulate and stream,
The mountains flow, the solids seem,
Change acts, reacts; back, forward hurled,
And pause were palsy to the world. —
The morn is come: the starry crowds
Are hid behind the thrice-piled clouds;
The new day lowers, and equal odds
Have changed not less the guest of gods;
Discrowned and timid, thoughtless, worn,
The child of genius sits forlorn:
Between two sleeps a short day's stealth,
'Mid many ails a brittle health,
A cripple of God, half true, half formed,
And by great sparks Promethean warmed,
Constrained by impotence to adjourn
To infinite time his eager turn,
His lot of action at the urn.

He by false usage pinned about
No breath therein, no passage out,
Cast wishful glances at the stars
And wishful saw the Ocean stream:—
'Merge me in the brute universe,
Or lift to a diviner dream!'

Beside him sat enduring love,
Upon him noble eyes did rest,
Which, for the Genius that there strove.
The follies bore that it invest.
They spoke not, for their earnest sense
Outran the craft of eloquence.

He whom God had thus preferred,—
To whom sweet angels ministered,
Saluted him each morn as brother,
And bragged his virtues to each other,—
Alas! how were they so beguiled,
And they so pure? He, foolish child,
A facile, reckless, wandering will,
Eager for good, not hating ill,
Thanked Nature for each stroke she dealt;
On his tense chords all strokes were felt,
The good, the bad with equal zeal,
He asked, he only asked, to feel.
Timid, self-pleasing, sensitive,
With Gods, with fools, content to live;
Bended to fops who bent to him;
Surface with surfaces did swim.

'Sorrow, sorrow!' the angels cried,
'Is this dear Nature's manly pride?
Call hither thy mortal enemy,
Make him glad thy fall to see!
Yon waterflag, yon sighing osier,

A drop can shake, a breath can fan;
Maidens laugh and weep; Composure
Is the pudency of man,'

Again by night the poet went
From the lighted halls
Beneath the darkling firmament
To the seashore, to the old seawalls,
Out shone a star beneath the cloud,
The constellation glittered soon, —
You have no lapse; so have ye glowed
But once in your dominion.
And yet, dear stars, I know ye shine
Only by needs and loves of mine;
Light-loving, light-asking life in me
Feeds those eternal lamps I see.
And I to whom your light has spoken,
I, pining to be one of you,
I fall, my faith is broken,
Ye scorn me from your deeps of blue.
Or if perchance, ye orbs of Fate,
Your ne'er averted glance
Beams with a will compassionate
On sons of time and chance,
Then clothe these hands with power
In just proportion,
Nor plant immense designs
Where equal means are none.'

CHORUS OF SPIRITS

Means, dear brother, ask them not;
Soul's desire is means enow,
Pure content is angel's lot,
Thine own theatre art thou.

Gentler far than falls the snow
In the woodwalks still and low
Fell the lesson on his heart
And woke the fear lest angels part.

POET

I see your forms with deep content,
I know that ye are excellent,
But will ye stay?
I hear the rustle of wings,
Ye meditate what to say
Ere ye go to quit me for ever and aye.

SPIRITS

Brother, we are no phantom band;
Brother, accept this fatal hand.
Aches thine unbelieving heart
With the fear that we must part?
See, all we are rooted here
By one thought to one same sphere;
From thyself thou canst not flee,—
From thyself no more can we.

POET

Suns and stars their courses keep,
But not angels of the deep:
Day and night their turn observe,
But the day of day may swerve.
Is there warrant that the waves
Of thought in their mysterious caves
Will heap in me their highest tide,
In me therewith beatified?
Unsure the ebb and flood of thought,
The moon comes back,—the Spirit not.

SPIRITS

Brother, sweeter is the Law
Than all the grace Love ever saw;
We are its suppliants. By it, we
Draw the breath of Eternity;
Serve thou it not for daily bread, —
Serve it for pain and fear and need.
Love it, though it hide its light;
By love behold the sun at night.
If the Law should thee forget,
More enamoured serve it yet;
Though it hate thee, suffer long;
Put the Spirit in the wrong;
Brother, no decrepitude
Chills the limbs of Time;
As fleet his feet, his hands as good,
His vision as sublime:
On Nature's wheels there is no rust;
Nor less on man's enchanted dust
Beauty and Force alight.

FRAGMENTS ON THE POET AND THE POETIC GIFT

I

There are beggars in Iran and Araby,
SAID was hungrier than all;
Hafiz said he was a fly
That came to every festival.
He came a pilgrim to the Mosque
On trail of camel and caravan,
Knew every temple and kiosk
Out from Mecca to Ispahan;
Northward he went to the snowy hills,
At court he sat in the grave Divan.
His music was the south-wind's sigh,
His lamp, the maiden's downcast eye,
And ever the spell of beauty came
And turned the drowsy world to flame.
By lake and stream and gleaming hall
And modest copse and the forest tall,
Where'er he went, the magic guide
Kept its place by the poet's side.
Said melted the days like cups of pearl,
Served high and low, the lord and the churl,
Loved harebells nodding on a rock,
A cabin hung with curling smoke,
Ring of axe or hum of wheel
Or gleam which use can paint on steel,
And huts and tents; nor loved he less
Stately lords in palaces,

Princely women hard to please,
Fenced by form and ceremony,
Decked by courtly rites and dress
And etiquette of gentilesse.
But when the mate of the snow and wind,
He left each civil scale behind:
Him wood-gods fed with honey wild
And of his memory beguiled.
He loved to watch and wake
When the wing of the south-wind whipt the lake
And the glassy surface in ripples brake
And fled in pretty frowns away
Like the flitting boreal lights,
Rippling roses in northern nights,
Or like the thrill of Aeolian strings
In which the sudden wind-god rings.
In caves and hollow trees he crept
And near the wolf and panther slept.
He came to the green ocean's brim
And saw the wheeling sea-birds skim,
Summer and winter, o'er the wave,
Like creatures of a skiey mould,
Impassible to heat or cold.
He stood before the tumbling main
With joy too tense for sober brain;
He shared the life of the element,
The tie of blood and home was rent:
As if in him the welkin walked,
The winds took flesh, the mountains talked,
And he the bard, a crystal soul
Sphered and concentric with the whole.
II

The Dervish whined to Said,
"Thou didst not tarry while I prayed.

Beware the fire that Eblis burned,"
But Saadi coldly thus returned,
"Once with manlike love and fear
I gave thee for an hour my ear,
I kept the sun and stars at bay,
And love, for words thy tongue could say.
I cannot sell my heaven again
For all that rattles in thy brain."
III

Said Saadi, "When I stood before
Hassan the camel-driver's door,
I scorned the fame of Timour brave;
Timour, to Hassan, was a slave.
In every glance of Hassan's eye
I read great years of victory,
And I, who cower mean and small
In the frequent interval
When wisdom not with me resides,
Worship Toil's wisdom that abides.
I shunned his eyes, that faithful man's,
I shunned the toiling Hassan's glance."
IV

The civil world will much forgive
To bards who from its maxims live,
But if, grown bold, the poet dare
Bend his practice to his prayer
And following his mighty heart
Shame the times and live apart, —
Vae solis! I found this,
That of goods I could not miss
If I fell within the line,
Once a member, all was mine,
Houses, banquets, gardens, fountains,

Fortune's delectable mountains;
But if I would walk alone,
Was neither cloak nor crumb my own.
And thus the high Muse treated me,
Directly never greeted me,
But when she spread her dearest spells,
Feigned to speak to some one else.
I was free to overhear,
Or I might at will forbear;
Yet mark me well, that idle word
Thus at random overheard
Was the symphony of spheres,
And proverb of a thousand years,
The light wherewith all planets shone,
The livery all events put on,
It fell in rain, it grew in grain,
It put on flesh in friendly form,
Frowned in my foe and growled in storm,
It spoke in Tullius Cicero,
In Milton and in Angelo:
I travelled and found it at Rome;
Eastward it filled all Heathendom
And it lay on my hearth when I came home.
V

Mask thy wisdom with delight,
Toy with the bow, yet hit the white,
As Jelaleddin old and gray;
He seemed to bask, to dream and play
Without remoter hope or fear
Than still to entertain his ear
And pass the burning summer-time
In the palm-grove with a rhyme;
Heedless that each cunning word
Tribes and ages overheard:

Those idle catches told the laws
Holding Nature to her cause.

God only knew how Saadi dined;
Roses he ate, and drank the wind;
He freelier breathed beside the pine,
In cities he was low and mean;
The mountain waters washed him clean
And by the sea-waves he was strong;
He heard their medicinal song,
Asked no physician but the wave,
No palace but his sea-beat cave.

Saadi held the Muse in awe,
She was his mistress and his law;
A twelvemonth he could silence hold,
Nor ran to speak till she him told;
He felt the flame, the fanning wings,
Nor offered words till they were things,
Glad when the solid mountain swims
In music and uplifting hymns.

Charmed from fagot and from steel,
Harvests grew upon his tongue,
Past and future must reveal
All their heart when Saadi sung;
Sun and moon must fall amain
Like sower's seeds into his brain,
There quickened to be born again.

The free winds told him what they knew,
Discoursed of fortune as they blew;
Omens and signs that filled the air
To him authentic witness bare;
The birds brought auguries on their wings,
And carolled undeceiving things

Him to beckon, him to warn;
Well might then the poet scorn
To learn of scribe or courier
Things writ in vaster character;
And on his mind at dawn of day
Soft shadows of the evening lay.
* * *

Pale genius roves alone,
No scout can track his way,
None credits him till he have shown
His diamonds to the day.

Not his the feaster's wine,
Nor land, nor gold, nor power,
By want and pain God screeneth him
Till his elected hour.

Go, speed the stars of Thought
On to their shining goals:—
The sower scatters broad his seed,
The wheat thou strew'st be souls.

I grieve that better souls than mine
Docile read my measured line:
High destined youths and holy maids
Hallow these my orchard shades;
Environ me and me baptize
With light that streams from gracious eyes.
I dare not be beloved and known,
I ungrateful, I alone.

Ever find me dim regards,
Love of ladies, love of bards,
Marked forbearance, compliments,
Tokens of benevolence.
What then, can I love myself?

Fame is profitless as pelf,
A good in Nature not allowed
They love me, as I love a cloud
Sailing falsely in the sphere,
Hated mist if it come near.

For thought, and not praise;
Thought is the wages
For which I sell days,
Will gladly sell ages
And willing grow old
Deaf, and dumb, and blind, and cold,
Melting matter into dreams,
Panoramas which I saw
And whatever glows or seems
Into substance, into Law.

For Fancy's gift
Can mountains lift;
The Muse can knit
What is past, what is done,
With the web that's just begun;
Making free with time and size,
Dwindles here, there magnifies,
Swells a rain-drop to a tun;
So to repeat
No word or feat
Crowds in a day the sum of ages,
And blushing Love outwits the sages.

Try the might the Muse affords
And the balm of thoughtful words;
Bring music to the desolate;
Hang roses on the stony fate.

But over all his crowning grace,

Wherefor thanks God his daily praise,
Is the purging of his eye
To see the people of the sky:
From blue mount and headland dim
Friendly hands stretch forth to him,
Him they beckon, him advise
Of heavenlier prosperities
And a more excelling grace
And a truer bosom-glow
Than the wine-fed feasters know.
They turn his heart from lovely maids,
And make the darlings of the earth
Swainish, coarse and nothing worth:
Teach him gladly to postpone
Pleasures to another stage
Beyond the scope of human age,
Freely as task at eve undone
Waits unblamed to-morrow's sun.

By thoughts I lead
Bards to say what nations need;
What imports, what irks and what behooves,
Framed afar as Fates and Loves.

And as the light divides the dark
Through with living swords,
So shall thou pierce the distant age
With adamantine words.

I framed his tongue to music,
I armed his hand with skill,
I moulded his face to beauty
And his heart the throne of Will.

For every God
Obeys the hymn, obeys the ode.

For art, for music over-thrilled,
The wine-cup shakes, the wine is spilled.

Hold of the Maker, not the Made;
Sit with the Cause, or grim or glad.

That book is good
Which puts me in a working mood.
Unless to Thought is added Will,
Apollo is an imbecile.
What parts, what gems, what colors shine,—
Ah, but I miss the grand design.

Like vaulters in a circus round
Who leap from horse to horse, but never touch the ground.

For Genius made his cabin wide,
And Love led Gods therein to bide.

The atom displaces all atoms beside,
And Genius unspheres all souls that abide.

To transmute crime to wisdom, so to stem
The vice of Japhet by the thought of Shem.

He could condense cerulean ether
Into the very best sole-leather.

Forbore the ant-hill, shunned to tread,
In mercy, on one little head.
I have no brothers and no peers,
And the dearest interferes:
When I would spend a lonely day,
Sun and moon are in my way.

The brook sings on, but sings in vain
Wanting the echo in my brain.

He planted where the deluge ploughed.

His hired hands were wind and cloud;
His eyes detect the Gods concealed
In the hummock of the field.

For what need I of book or priest,
Or sibyl from the mummied East,
When every star is Bethlehem star?
I count as many as there are
Cinquefoils or violets in the grass,
So many saints and saviors,
So many high behaviors
Salute the bard who is alive
And only sees what he doth give.

Coin the day-dawn into lines
In which its proper splendor shines;
Coin the moonlight into verse
Which all its marvel shall rehearse,
Chasing with words fast-flowing things; nor try
To plant thy shrivelled pedantry
On the shoulders of the sky.

Ah, not to me those dreams belong!
A better voice peals through my song.

The Muse's hill by Fear is guarded,
A bolder foot is still rewarded.

His instant thought a poet spoke,
And filled the age his fame;
An inch of ground the lightning strook
But lit the sky with flame.

If bright the sun, he tarries,
All day his song is heard;
And when he goes he carries

No more baggage than a bird.

The Asmodean feat is mine,
To spin my sand-heap into twine.

Slighted Minerva's learnèd tongue,
But leaped with joy when on the wind
The shell of Clio rung.

FRAGMENTS ON NATURE AND LIFE

NATURE

The patient Pan,
Drunken with nectar,
Sleeps or feigns slumber,
Drowsily humming
Music to the march of time.
This poor tooting, creaking cricket,
Pan, half asleep, rolling over
His great body in the grass,
Tooting, creaking,
Feigns to sleep, sleeping never;
'T is his manner,
Well he knows his own affair,
Piling mountain chains of phlegm
On the nervous brain of man,
As he holds down central fires
Under Alps and Andes cold;
Haply else we could not live,
Life would be too wild an ode.

Come search the wood for flowers,—
Wild tea and wild pea,
Grapevine and succory,
Coreopsis
And liatris,
Flaunting in their bowers;
Grass with green flag half-mast high,

Succory to match the sky,
Columbine with horn of honey,
Scented fern and agrimony;
Forest full of essences
Fit for fairy presences,
Peppermint and sassafras,
Sweet fern, mint and vernal grass,
Panax, black birch, sugar maple,
Sweet and scent for Dian's table,
Elder-blow, sarsaparilla,
Wild rose, lily, dry vanilla,—
Spices in the plants that run
To bring their first fruits to the sun.
Earliest heats that follow frore
Nervèd leaf of hellebore,
Sweet willow, checkerberry red,
With its savory leaf for bread.
Silver birch and black
With the selfsame spice
Found in polygala root and rind,
Sassafras, fern, benzöine,
Mouse-ear, cowslip, wintergreen,
Which by aroma may compel
The frost to spare, what scents so well.

Where the fungus broad and red
Lifts its head,
Like poisoned loaf of elfin bread,
Where the aster grew
With the social goldenrod,
In a chapel, which the dew
Made beautiful for God:—
O what would Nature say?
She spared no speech to-day:
The fungus and the bulrush spoke,

Answered the pine-tree and the oak,
The wizard South blew down the glen,
Filled the straits and filled the wide,
Each maple leaf turned up its silver side.
All things shine in his smoky ray,
And all we see are pictures high;
Many a high hillside,
While oaks of pride
Climb to their tops,
And boys run out upon their leafy ropes.
The maple street
In the houseless wood,
Voices followed after,
Every shrub and grape leaf
Rang with fairy laughter.
I have heard them fall
Like the strain of all
King Oberon's minstrelsy.
Would hear the everlasting
And know the only strong?
You must worship fasting,
You must listen long.
Words of the air
Which birds of the air
Carry aloft, below, around,
To the isles of the deep,
To the snow-capped steep,
To the thundercloud.

For Nature, true and like in every place,
Will hint her secret in a garden patch,
Or in lone corners of a doleful heath,
As in the Andes watched by fleets at sea,
Or the sky-piercing horns of Himmaleh;
And, when I would recall the scenes I dreamed

On Adirondac steeps, I know
Small need have I of Turner or Daguerre,
Assured to find the token once again
In silver lakes that unexhausted gleam
And peaceful woods beside my cottage door.

What all the books of ages paint, I have.
What prayers and dreams of youthful genius feign,
I daily dwell in, and am not so blind
But I can see the elastic tent of day
Belike has wider hospitality
Than my few needs exhaust, and bids me read
The quaint devices on its mornings gay.
Yet Nature will not be in full possessed,
And they who truliest love her, heralds are
And harbingers of a majestic race,
Who, having more absorbed, more largely yield,
And walk on earth as the sun walks in the sphere.

But never yet the man was found
Who could the mystery expound,
Though Adam, born when oaks were young,
Endured, the Bible says, as long;
But when at last the patriarch died
The Gordian noose was still untied.
He left, though goodly centuries old,
Meek Nature's secret still untold.

Atom from atom yawns as far
As moon from earth, or star from star.

When all their blooms the meadows flaunt
To deck the morning of the year,
Why tinge thy lustres jubilant
With forecast or with fear?

Teach me your mood, O patient stars!

Who climb each night the ancient sky,
Leaving on space no shade, no scars,
No trace of age, no fear to die.

The sun athwart the cloud thought it no sin
To use my land to put his rainbows in.

For joy and beauty planted it,
With faerie gardens cheered,
And boding Fancy haunted it
With men and women weird.

What central flowing forces, say,
Make up thy splendor, matchless day?

Day by day for her darlings to her much she added more;
In her hundred-gated Thebes every chamber was a door,
A door to something grander,—loftier walls, and vaster
floor.

She paints with white and red the moors
To draw the nations out of doors.
A score of airy miles will smooth
Rough Monadnoc to a gem.

THE EARTH

Our eyeless bark sails free
Though with boom and spar
Andes, Alp or Himmalee,
Strikes never moon or star.

THE HEAVENS

Wisp and meteor nightly falling,
But the Stars of God remain.

TRANSITION

See yonder leafless trees against the sky,
How they diffuse themselves into the air,
And, ever subdividing, separate
Limbs into branches, branches into twigs.
As if they loved the element, and hasted
To dissipate their being into it.

Parks and ponds are good by day;
I do not delight
In black acres of the night,
Nor my unseasoned step disturbs
The sleeps of trees or dreams of herbs.

In Walden wood the chickadee
Runs round the pine and maple tree
Intent on insect slaughter:
O tufted entomologist!
Devour as many as you list,
Then drink in Walden water.

The low December vault in June be lifted high,
And largest clouds be flakes of down in that enormous sky.

THE GARDEN

Many things the garden shows,
And pleased I stray
From tree to tree
Watching the white pear-bloom,
Bee-infested quince or plum.
I could walk days, years, away
Till the slow ripening, secular tree
Had reached its fruiting-time,
Nor think it long.

Solar insect on the wing
In the garden murmuring,
Soothing with thy summer horn
Swains by winter pinched and worn.

BIRDS

Darlings of children and of bard,
Perfect kinds by vice unmarred,
All of worth and beauty set
Gems in Nature's cabinet;
These the fables she esteems
Reality most like to dreams.
Welcome back, you little nations,
Far-travelled in the south plantations;
Bring your music and rhythmic flight,
Your colors for our eyes' delight:
Freely nestle in our roof,
Weave your chamber weatherproof;
And your enchanting manners bring
And your autumnal gathering.
Exchange in conclave general
Greetings kind to each and all,
Conscious each of duty done
And unstainèd as the sun.

WATER

The water understands
Civilization well;
It wets my foot, but prettily
It chills my life, but wittily,
It is not disconcerted,
It is not broken-hearted:
Well used, it decketh joy,
Adorneth, doubleth joy:
Ill used, it will destroy,
In perfect time and measure
With a face of golden pleasure
Elegantly destroy.

NAHANT

All day the waves assailed the rock,
I heard no church-bell chime,
The sea-beat scorns the minster clock
And breaks the glass of Time.

SUNRISE

Would you know what joy is hid
In our green Musketaquid,
And for travelled eyes what charms
Draw us to these meadow farms,
Come and I will show you all
Makes each day a festival.
Stand upon this pasture hill,
Face the eastern star until
The slow eye of heaven shall show
The world above, the world below.

Behold the miracle!
Thou saw'st but now the twilight sad
And stood beneath the firmament,
A watchman in a dark gray tent,
Waiting till God create the earth,—
Behold the new majestic birth!
The mottled clouds, like scraps of wool,
Steeped in the light are beautiful.
What majestic stillness broods
Over these colored solitudes.
Sleeps the vast East in pleasèd peace,
Up the far mountain walls the streams increase
Inundating the heaven
With spouting streams and waves of light
Which round the floating isles unite:—
See the world below
Baptized with the pure element,

A clear and glorious firmament
Touched with life by every beam.
I share the good with every flower,
I drink the nectar of the hour:—
This is not the ancient earth
Whereof old chronicles relate
The tragic tales of crime and fate;
But rather, like its beads of dew
And dew-bent violets, fresh and new,
An exhalation of the time.

* * *

NIGHT IN JUNE

I left my dreary page and sallied forth,
Received the fair inscriptions of the night;
The moon was making amber of the world,
Glittered with silver every cottage pane,
The trees were rich, yet ominous with gloom.
The meadows broad
From ferns and grapes and from the folded flowers
Sent a nocturnal fragrance; harlot flies
Flashed their small fires in air, or held their court
In fairy groves of herds-grass.

He lives not who can refuse me;
All my force saith, Come and use me:
A gleam of sun, a summer rain,
And all the zone is green again.

Seems, though the soft sheen all enchants,
Cheers the rough crag and mournful dell,
As if on such stern forms and haunts
A wintry storm more fitly fell.

Put in, drive home the sightless wedges
And split to flakes the crystal ledges.

MAIA

Illusion works impenetrable,
Weaving webs innumerable,
Her gay pictures never fail,
Crowds each on other, veil on veil,
Charmer who will be believed
By man who thirsts to be deceived.

Illusions like the tints of pearl,
Or changing colors of the sky,
Or ribbons of a dancing girl
That mend her beauty to the eye.

The cold gray down upon the quinces lieth
And the poor spinners weave their webs thereon
To share the sunshine that so spicy is.

Samson stark, at Dagon's knee,
Gropes for columns strong as he;
When his ringlets grew and curled,
Groped for axle of the world.

But Nature whistled with all her winds,
Did as she pleased and went her way.

LIFE

A train of gay and clouded days
Dappled with joy and grief and praise,
Beauty to fire us, saints to save,
Escort us to a little grave.

No fate, save by the victim's fault, is low,
For God hath writ all dooms magnificent,
So guilt not traverses his tender will.

Around the man who seeks a noble end,
Not angels but divinities attend.

From high to higher forces
The scale of power uprears,
The heroes on their horses,
The gods upon their spheres.

This shining moment is an edifice
Which the Omnipotent cannot rebuild.

Roomy Eternity
Casts her schemes rarely,
And an aeon allows
For each quality and part
Of the multitudinous
And many-chambered heart.

The beggar begs by God's command,
And gifts awake when givers sleep,
Swords cannot cut the giving hand
Nor stab the love that orphans keep.

In the chamber, on the stairs,
Lurking dumb,
Go and come
Lemurs and Lars.

Such another peerless queen
Only could her mirror show.

Easy to match what others do,
Perform the feat as well as they;
Hard to out-do the brave, the true,
And find a loftier way:
The school decays, the learning spoils
Because of the sons of wine;
How snatch the stripling from their toils?—
Yet can one ray of truth divine
The blaze of revellers' feasts outshine.

Of all wit's uses the main one
Is to live well with who has none.

The tongue is prone to lose the way,
Not so the pen, for in a letter
We have not better things to say,
But surely say them better.

She walked in flowers around my field
As June herself around the sphere.

Friends to me are frozen wine;
I wait the sun on them should shine.

You shall not love me for what daily spends;
You shall not know me in the noisy street,
Where I, as others, follow petty ends;
Nor when in fair saloons we chance to meet;
Nor when I'm jaded, sick, anxious or mean.
But love me then and only, when you know

Me for the channel of the rivers of God
From deep ideal fontal heavens that flow.

To and fro the Genius flies,
A light which plays and hovers
Over the maiden's head
And dips sometimes as low as to her eyes.
Of her faults I take no note,
Fault and folly are not mine;
Comes the Genius,—all's forgot,
Replunged again into that upper sphere
He scatters wide and wild its lustres here.

Love
Asks nought his brother cannot give;
Asks nothing, but does all receive.
Love calls not to his aid events;
He to his wants can well suffice:
Asks not of others soft consents,
Nor kind occasion without eyes;
Nor plots to ope or bolt a gate,
Nor heeds Condition's iron walls,—
Where he goes, goes before him Fate;
Whom he uniteth, God installs;
Instant and perfect his access
To the dear object of his thought,
Though foes and land and seas between
Himself and his love intervene.

The brave Empedocles, defying fools,
Pronounced the word that mortals hate to hear—
"I am divine, I am not mortal made;
I am superior to my human weeds."
Not Sense but Reason is the Judge of truth;
Reason's twofold, part human, part divine;
That human part may be described and taught,

The other portion language cannot speak.

Tell men what they knew before;
Paint the prospect from their door.

Him strong Genius urged to roam,
Stronger Custom brought him home.

That each should in his house abide.
Therefore was the world so wide.

Thou shalt make thy house
The temple of a nation's vows.
Spirits of a higher strain
Who sought thee once shall seek again.
I detected many a god
Forth already on the road,
Ancestors of beauty come
In thy breast to make a home.

The archangel Hope
Looks to the azure cope,
Waits through dark ages for the morn,
Defeated day by day, but unto victory born.
As the drop feeds its fated flower,
As finds its Alp the snowy shower,
Child of the omnific Need,
Hurled into life to do a deed,
Man drinks the water, drinks the light.

Ever the Rock of Ages melts
Into the mineral air,
To be the quarry whence to build
Thought and its mansions fair.

Go if thou wilt, ambrosial flower,
Go match thee with thy seeming peers;
I will wait Heaven's perfect hour

Through the innumerable years.

Yes, sometimes to the sorrow-stricken
Shall his own sorrow seem impertinent,
A thing that takes no more root in the world
Than doth the traveller's shadow on the rock.

But if thou do thy best,
Without remission, without rest,
And invite the sunbeam,
And abhor to feign or seem
Even to those who thee should love
And thy behavior approve;
If thou go in thine own likeness,
Be it health, or be it sickness;
If thou go as thy father's son,
If thou wear no mask or lie,
Dealing purely and nakedly, —
* * *

Ascending thorough just degrees
To a consummate holiness,
As angel blind to trespass done,
And bleaching all souls like the sun.

From the stores of eldest matter,
The deep-eyed flame, obedient water,
Transparent air, all-feeding earth,
He took the flower of all their worth,
And, best with best in sweet consent,
Combined a new temperament.

REX

The bard and mystic held me for their own,
I filled the dream of sad, poetic maids,
I took the friendly noble by the hand,
I was the trustee of the hand-cart man,
The brother of the fisher, porter, swain,
And these from the crowd's edge well pleased beheld
The service done to me as done to them.

With the key of the secret he marches faster,
From strength to strength, and for night brings day;
While classes or tribes, too weak to master
The flowing conditions of life, give way.

SUUM CUIQUE

Wilt thou seal up the avenues of ill?
Pay every debt as if God wrote the bill.

If curses be the wage of love,
Hide in thy skies, thou fruitless Jove,
Not to be named:
It is clear
Why the gods will not appear;
They are ashamed.

When wrath and terror changed Jove's regal port,
And the rash-leaping thunderbolt fell short.

Shun passion, fold the hands of thrift,
Sit still and Truth is near:
Suddenly it will uplift
Your eyelids to the sphere:
Wait a little, you shall see
The portraiture of things to be.

The rules to men made evident
By Him who built the day,
The columns of the firmament
Not firmer based than they.

On bravely through the sunshine and the showers!
Time hath his work to do and we have ours.

THE BOHEMIAN HYMN

In many forms we try
To utter God's infinity,
But the boundless hath no form,
And the Universal Friend
Doth as far transcend
An angel as a worm.

The great Idea baffles wit,
Language falters under it,
It leaves the learned in the lurch;
Nor art, nor power, nor toil can find
The measure of the eternal Mind,
Nor hymn, nor prayer, nor church.

GRACE

How much, preventing God, how much I owe
To the defences thou hast round me set;
Example, custom, fear, occasion slow, —
These scorned bondmen were my parapet.
I dare not peep over this parapet
To gauge with glance the roaring gulf below,
The depths of sin to which I had descended,
Had not these me against myself defended.

INSIGHT

Power that by obedience grows,
Knowledge which its source not knows,
Wave which severs whom it bears
From the things which he compares,
Adding wings through things to range,
To his own blood harsh and strange.

PAN

O what are heroes, prophets, men,
But pipes through which the breath of Pan doth blow
A momentary music. Being's tide
Swells hitherward, and myriads of forms
Live, robed with beauty, painted by the sun;
Their dust, pervaded by the nerves of God,
Throbs with an overmastering energy
Knowing and doing. Ebbs the tide, they lie
White hollow shells upon the desert shore,
But not the less the eternal wave rolls on
To animate new millions, and exhale
Races and planets, its enchanted foam.

MONADNOC FROM AFAR

Dark flower of Cheshire garden,
Red evening duly dyes
Thy sombre head with rosy hues
To fix far-gazing eyes.
Well the Planter knew how strongly
Works thy form on human thought;
I muse what secret purpose had he
To draw all fancies to this spot.

SEPTEMBER

In the turbulent beauty
Of a gusty Autumn day,
Poet on a sunny headland
Sighed his soul away.

Farms the sunny landscape dappled,
Swandown clouds dappled the farms,
Cattle lowed in mellow distance
Where far oaks outstretched their arms.

Sudden gusts came full of meaning,
All too much to him they said,
Oh, south winds have long memories,
Of that be none afraid.

I cannot tell rude listeners
Half the tell-tale South-wind said,—
'T would bring the blushes of yon maples
To a man and to a maid.

EROS

They put their finger on their lip,
The Powers above:
The seas their islands clip,
The moons in ocean dip,
They love, but name not love.

OCTOBER

October woods wherein
The boy's dream comes to pass,
And Nature squanders on the boy her pomp,
And crowns him with a more than royal crown,
And unimagined splendor waits his steps.
The gazing urchin walks through tents of gold,
Through crimson chambers, porphyry and pearl,
Pavilion on pavilion, garlanded,
Incensed and starred with lights and airs and shapes,
Color and sound, music to eye and ear,
Beyond the best conceit of pomp or power.

PETER'S FIELD

[Knows he who tills this lonely field
To reap its scanty corn,
What mystic fruit his acres yield
At midnight and at morn?]

That field by spirits bad and good,
By Hell and Heaven is haunted,
And every rood in the hemlock wood
I know is ground enchanted.

[In the long sunny afternoon
The plain was full of ghosts:
I wandered up, I wandered down,
Beset by pensive hosts.]

For in those lonely grounds the sun
Shines not as on the town,
In nearer arcs his journeys run,
And nearer stoops the moon.

There in a moment I have seen
The buried Past arise;
The fields of Thessaly grew green,
Old gods forsook the skies.

I cannot publish in my rhyme
What pranks the greenwood played;
It was the Carnival of time,
And Ages went or stayed.

To me that spectral nook appeared

The mustering Day of Doom,
And round me swarmed in shadowy troop
Things past and things to come.

The darkness haunteth me elsewhere;
There I am full of light;
In every whispering leaf I hear
More sense than sages write.

Underwoods were full of pleasance,
All to each in kindness bend,
And every flower made obeisance
As a man unto his friend.

Far seen, the river glides below,
Tossing one sparkle to the eyes:
I catch thy meaning, wizard wave;
The River of my Life replies.

MUSIC

Let me go where'er I will,
I hear a sky-born music still:
It sounds from all things old,
It sounds from all things young,
From all that's fair, from all that's foul,
Peals out a cheerful song.

It is not only in the rose,
It is not only in the bird,
Not only where the rainbow glows,
Nor in the song of woman heard,
But in the darkest, meanest things
There alway, alway something sings.

'T is not in the high stars alone,
Nor in the cup of budding flowers,
Nor in the redbreast's mellow tone,
Nor in the bow that smiles in showers,
But in the mud and scum of things
There alway, alway something sings.

THE WALK

A Queen rejoices in her peers,
And wary Nature knows her own
By court and city, dale and down,
And like a lover volunteers,
And to her son will treasures more
And more to purpose freely pour
In one wood walk, than learned men
Can find with glass in ten times ten.

COSMOS

Who saw the hid beginnings
When Chaos and Order strove,
Or who can date the morning.
The purple flaming of love?

I saw the hid beginnings
When Chaos and Order strove,
And I can date the morning prime
And purple flame of love.

Song breathed from all the forest,
The total air was fame;
It seemed the world was all torches
That suddenly caught the flame.
* * *

Is there never a retroscope mirror
In the realms and corners of space
That can give us a glimpse of the battle
And the soldiers face to face?

Sit here on the basalt courses
Where twisted hills betray
The seat of the world-old Forces
Who wrestled here on a day.
* * *

When the purple flame shoots up,
And Love ascends his throne,
I cannot hear your songs, O birds,

For the witchery of my own.

And every human heart
Still keeps that golden day
And rings the bells of jubilee
On its own First of May.

THE MIRACLE

I have trod this path a hundred times
With idle footsteps, crooning rhymes.
I know each nest and web-worm's tent,
The fox-hole which the woodchucks rent,
Maple and oak, the old Divan
Self-planted twice, like the banian.
I know not why I came again
Unless to learn it ten times ten.
To read the sense the woods impart
You must bring the throbbing heart.
Love is aye the counterforce, —
Terror and Hope and wild Remorse,
Newest knowledge, fiery thought,
Or Duty to grand purpose wrought.
Wandering yester morn the brake,
I reached this heath beside the lake,
And oh, the wonder of the power,
The deeper secret of the hour!
Nature, the supplement of man,
His hidden sense interpret can; —
What friend to friend cannot convey
Shall the dumb bird instructed say.
Passing yonder oak, I heard
Sharp accents of my woodland bird;
I watched the singer with delight, —
But mark what changed my joy to fright, —
When that bird sang, I gave the theme;
That wood-bird sang my last night's dream,

A brown wren was the Daniel
That pierced my trance its drift to tell,
Knew my quarrel, how and why,
Published it to lake and sky,
Told every word and syllable
In his flippant chirping babble,
All my wrath and all my shames,
Nay, God is witness, gave the names.

THE WATERFALL

A patch of meadow upland
Reached by a mile of road,
Soothed by the voice of waters,
With birds and flowers bestowed.

Hither I come for strength
Which well it can supply,
For Love draws might from terrene force
And potencies of sky.

The tremulous battery Earth
Responds to the touch of man;
It thrills to the antipodes,
From Boston to Japan.

The planets' child the planet knows
And to his joy replies;
To the lark's trill unfolds the rose,
Clouds flush their gayest dyes.

When Ali prayed and loved
Where Syrian waters roll,
Upward the ninth heaven thrilled and moved;
At the tread of the jubilant soul.

WALDEN

In my garden three ways meet,
Thrice the spot is blest;
Hermit-thrush comes there to build,
Carrier-doves to nest.

There broad-armed oaks, the copses' maze,
The cold sea-wind detain;
Here sultry Summer overstays
When Autumn chills the plain.

Self-sown my stately garden grows;
The winds and wind-blown seed,
Cold April rain and colder snows
My hedges plant and feed.

From mountains far and valleys near
The harvests sown to-day
Thrive in all weathers without fear, —
Wild planters, plant away!

In cities high the careful crowds
Of woe-worn mortals darkling go,
But in these sunny solitudes
My quiet roses blow.

Methought the sky looked scornful down
On all was base in man,
And airy tongues did taunt the town,
'Achieve our peace who can!'

What need I holier dew
Than Walden's haunted wave,

Distilled from heaven's alembic blue,
Steeped in each forest cave?

[If Thought unlock her mysteries,
If Friendship on me smile,
I walk in marble galleries,
I talk with kings the while.]

How drearily in College hall
The Doctor stretched the hours,
But in each pause we heard the call
Of robins out of doors.

The air is wise, the wind thinks well,
And all through which it blows,
If plants or brain, if egg or shell,
Or bird or biped knows;

And oft at home 'mid tasks I heed,
I heed how wears the day;
We must not halt while fiercely speed
The spans of life away.

What boots it here of Thebes or Rome
Or lands of Eastern day?
In forests I am still at home
And there I cannot stray.

THE ENCHANTER

In the deep heart of man a poet dwells
Who all the day of life his summer story tells;
Scatters on every eye dust of his spells,
Scent, form and color; to the flowers and shells
Wins the believing child with wondrous tales;
Touches a cheek with colors of romance,
And crowds a history into a glance;
Gives beauty to the lake and fountain,
Spies oversea the fires of the mountain;
When thrushes ope their throat, 't is he that sings,
And he that paints the oriole's fiery wings.
The little Shakspeare in the maiden's heart
Makes Romeo of a plough-boy on his cart;
Opens the eye to Virtue's starlike meed
And gives persuasion to a gentle deed.

WRITTEN IN A VOLUME OF GOETHE

Six thankful weeks,—and let it be
A meter of prosperity,—
In my coat I bore this book,
And seldom therein could I look,
For I had too much to think,
Heaven and earth to eat and drink.
Is he hapless who can spare
In his plenty things so rare?

RICHES

Have ye seen the caterpillar
Foully warking in his nest?
'T is the poor man getting siller,
Without cleanness, without rest.

Have ye seen the butterfly
In braw claithing drest?
'T is the poor man gotten rich,
In rings and painted vest.

The poor man crawls in web of rags
And sore bested with woes.
But when he flees on riches' wings,
He laugheth at his foes.

PHILOSOPHER

Philosophers are lined with eyes within,
And, being so, the sage unmakes the man.
In love, he cannot therefore cease his trade;
Scarce the first blush has overspread his cheek,
He feels it, introverts his learned eye
To catch the unconscious heart in the very act.

His mother died,—the only friend he had,—
Some tears escaped, but his philosophy
Couched like a cat sat watching close behind
And throttled all his passion. Is't not like
That devil-spider that devours her mate
Scarce freed from her embraces?

INTELLECT

Gravely it broods apart on joy,
And, truth to tell, amused by pain.

LIMITS

Who knows this or that?
Hark in the wall to the rat:
Since the world was, he has gnawed;
Of his wisdom, of his fraud
What dost thou know?
In the wretched little beast
Is life and heart,
Child and parent,
Not without relation
To fruitful field and sun and moon.
What art thou? His wicked eye
Is cruel to thy cruelty.

INSCRIPTION FOR A WELL IN MEMORY OF THE MARTYRS OF THE WAR

Fall, stream, from Heaven to bless; return as well;
So did our sons; Heaven met them as they fell.

THE EXILE

(AFTER TALIESSIN)

The heavy blue chain
Of the boundless main
Didst thou, just man, endure.

I have an arrow that will find its mark,
A mastiff that will bite without a hark.

VI
POEMS OF YOUTH AND EARLY MANHOOD

1823-1834

THE BELL

I love thy music, mellow bell,
I love thine iron chime,
To life or death, to heaven or hell,
Which calls the sons of Time.

Thy voice upon the deep
The home-bound sea-boy hails,
It charms his cares to sleep,
It cheers him as he sails.

To house of God and heavenly joys
Thy summons called our sires,
And good men thought thy sacred voice
Disarmed the thunder's fires.

And soon thy music, sad death-bell,
Shall lift its notes once more,
And mix my requiem with the wind
That sweeps my native shore.
1823.

THOUGHT

I am not poor, but I am proud,
Of one inalienable right,
Above the envy of the crowd, —
Thought's holy light.

Better it is than gems or gold,
And oh! it cannot die,
But thought will glow when the sun grows cold,
And mix with Deity.
BOSTON, 1823.

PRAYER

When success exalts thy lot,
God for thy virtue lays a plot:
And all thy life is for thy own,
Then for mankind's instruction shown;
And though thy knees were never bent,
To Heaven thy hourly prayers are sent,
And whether formed for good or ill,
Are registered and answered still.

1826 [?].
I bear in youth the sad infirmities
That use to undo the limb and sense of age;
It hath pleased Heaven to break the dream of bliss
Which lit my onward way with bright presage,
And my unserviceable limbs forego.
The sweet delight I found in fields and farms,
On windy hills, whose tops with morning glow,
And lakes, smooth mirrors of Aurora's charms.
Yet I think on them in the silent night,
Still breaks that morn, though dim, to Memory's eye,
And the firm soul does the pale train defy
Of grim Disease, that would her peace affright.
Please God, I'll wrap me in mine innocence,
And bid each awful Muse drive the damned harpies hence.

CAMBRIDGE, 1827.

Be of good cheer, brave spirit; steadfastly
Serve that low whisper thou hast served; for know,
God hath a select family of sons

Now scattered wide thro' earth, and each alone,
Who are thy spiritual kindred, and each one
By constant service to, that inward law,
Is weaving the sublime proportions
Of a true monarch's soul. Beauty and strength,
The riches of a spotless memory,
The eloquence of truth, the wisdom got
By searching of a clear and loving eye
That seeth as God seeth. These are their gifts,
And Time, who keeps God's word, brings on the day
To seal the marriage of these minds with thine,
Thine everlasting lovers. Ye shall be
The salt of all the elements, world of the world.

TO-DAY

I rake no coffined clay, nor publish wide
The resurrection of departed pride.
Safe in their ancient crannies, dark and deep,
Let kings and conquerors, saints and soldiers sleep—
Late in the world,—too late perchance for fame,
Just late enough to reap abundant blame,—
I choose a novel theme, a bold abuse
Of critic charters, an unlaurelled Muse.

Old mouldy men and books and names and lands
Disgust my reason and defile my hands.
I had as lief respect an ancient shoe,
As love old things *for age*, and hate the new.
I spurn the Past, my mind disdains its nod,
Nor kneels in homage to so mean a God.
I laugh at those who, while they gape and gaze,
The bald antiquity of China praise.
Youth is (whatever cynic tubs pretend)
The fault that boys and nations soonest mend.
1824.

FAME

Ah Fate, cannot a man
Be wise without a beard?
East, West, from Beer to Dan,
Say, was it never heard
That wisdom might in youth be gotten,
Or wit be ripe before 't was rotten?

He pays too high a price
For knowledge and for fame
Who sells his sinews to be wise,
His teeth and bones to buy a name,
And crawls through life a paralytic
To earn the praise of bard and critic.

Were it not better done,
To dine and sleep through forty years;
Be loved by few; be feared by none;
Laugh life away; have wine for tears;
And take the mortal leap undaunted,
Content that all we asked was granted?

But Fate will not permit
The seed of gods to die,
Nor suffer sense to win from wit
Its guerdon in the sky,
Nor let us hide, whate'er our pleasure,
The world's light underneath a measure.

Go then, sad youth, and shine;
Go, sacrifice to Fame;

Put youth, joy, health upon the shrine,
And life to fan the flame;
Being for Seeming bravely barter
And die to Fame a happy martyr.
1824.

THE SUMMONS

A sterner errand to the silken troop
Has quenched the uneasy blush that warmed my cheek;
I am commissioned in my day of joy
To leave my woods and streams and the sweet sloth
Of prayer and song that were my dear delight,
To leave the rudeness of my woodland life,
Sweet twilight walks and midnight solitude
And kind acquaintance with the morning stars
And the glad hey-day of my household hours,
The innocent mirth which sweetens daily bread,
Railing in love to those who rail again,
By mind's industry sharpening the love of life—
Books, Muses, Study, fireside, friends and love,
I loved ye with true love, so fare ye well!

I was a boy; boyhood slid gayly by
And the impatient years that trod on it
Taught me new lessons in the lore of life.
I've learned the sum of that sad history
All woman-born do know, that hoped-for days,
Days that come dancing on fraught with delights,
Dash our blown hopes as they limp heavily by.
But I, the bantling of a country Muse,
Abandon all those toys with speed to obey
The King whose meek ambassador I go.
1826.

THE RIVER

And I behold once more
My old familiar haunts; here the blue river,
The same blue wonder that my infant eye
Admired, sage doubting whence the traveller came, —
Whence brought his sunny bubbles ere he washed
The fragrant flag-roots in my father's fields,
And where thereafter in the world he went.
Look, here he is, unaltered, save that now
He hath broke his banks and flooded all the vales
With his redundant waves.
Here is the rock where, yet a simple child,
I caught with bended pin my earliest fish,
Much triumphing, — and these the fields
Over whose flowers I chased the butterfly
A blooming hunter of a fairy fine.
And hark! where overhead the ancient crows
Hold their sour conversation in the sky: —
These are the same, but I am not the same,
But wiser than I was, and wise enough
Not to regret the changes, tho' they cost
Me many a sigh. Oh, call not Nature dumb;
These trees and stones are audible to me,
These idle flowers, that tremble in the wind,
I understand their faery syllables,
And all their sad significance. The wind,
That rustles down the well-known forest road —
It hath a sound more eloquent than speech.
The stream, the trees, the grass, the sighing wind,

All of them utter sounds of 'monishment
And grave parental love.
They are not of our race, they seem to say,
And yet have knowledge of our moral race,
And somewhat of majestic sympathy,
Something of pity for the puny clay,
That holds and boasts the immeasurable mind.
I feel as I were welcome to these trees
After long months of weary wandering,
Acknowledged by their hospitable boughs;
They know me as their son, for side by side,
They were coeval with my ancestors,
Adorned with them my country's primitive times,
And soon may give my dust their funeral shade.

CONCORD, June, 1827.

GOOD HOPE

The cup of life is not so shallow
That we have drained the best,
That all the wine at once we swallow
And lees make all the rest.

Maids of as soft a bloom shall marry
As Hymen yet hath blessed,
And fairer forms are in the quarry
Than Phidias released.
1827.

LINES TO ELLEN

Tell me, maiden, dost thou use
Thyself thro' Nature to diffuse?
All the angles of the coast
Were tenanted by thy sweet ghost,
Bore thy colors every flower,
Thine each leaf and berry bore;
All wore thy badges and thy favors
In their scent or in their savors,
Every moth with painted wing,
Every bird in carolling,
The wood-boughs with thy manners waved,
The rocks uphold thy name engraved,
The sod throbbed friendly to my feet,
And the sweet air with thee was sweet.
The saffron cloud that floated warm
Studied thy motion, took thy form,
And in his airy road benign
Recalled thy skill in bold design,
Or seemed to use his privilege
To gaze o'er the horizon's edge,
To search where now thy beauty glowed,
Or made what other purlieus proud.
1829.

SECURITY

Though her eye seek other forms
And a glad delight below,
Yet the love the world that warms
Bids for me her bosom glow.

She must love me till she find
Another heart as large and true.
Her soul is frank as the ocean wind,
And the world has only two.

If Nature hold another heart
That knows a purer flame than me,
I too therein could challenge part
And learn of love a new degree.
1829.

A dull uncertain brain,
But gifted yet to know
That God has cherubim who go
Singing an immortal strain,
Immortal here below.
I know the mighty bards,
I listen when they sing,
And now I know
The secret store
Which these explore
When they with torch of genius pierce
The tenfold clouds that cover
The riches of the universe

From God's adoring lover.
And if to me it is not given
To fetch one ingot thence
Of the unfading gold of Heaven
His merchants may dispense,
Yet well I know the royal mine,
And know the sparkle of its ore,
Know Heaven's truth from lies that shine—
Explored they teach us to explore.
1831.

A MOUNTAIN GRAVE

Why fear to die
And let thy body lie
Under the flowers of June,
Thy body food
For the ground-worms' brood
And thy grave smiled on by the visiting moon.

Amid great Nature's halls
Girt in by mountain walls
And washed with waterfalls
It would please me to die,
Where every wind that swept my tomb
Goes loaded with a free perfume
Dealt out with a God's charity.

I should like to die in sweets,
A hill's leaves for winding-sheets,
And the searching sun to see
That I am laid with decency.
And the commissioned wind to sing
His mighty psalm from fall to spring
And annual tunes commemorate
Of Nature's child the common fate.

WILLIAMSTOWN, VERMONT, 1 June, 1831.

A LETTER

Dear brother, would you know the life,
Please God, that I would lead?
On the first wheels that quit this weary town
Over yon western bridges I would ride
And with a cheerful benison forsake
Each street and spire and roof, incontinent.
Then would I seek where God might guide my steps,
Deep in a woodland tract, a sunny farm,
Amid the mountain counties, Hants, Franklin, Berks,
Where down the rock ravine a river roars,
Even from a brook, and where old woods
Not tamed and cleared cumber the ground
With their centennial wrecks.
Find me a slope where I can feel the sun
And mark the rising of the early stars.
There will I bring my books, —my household gods,
The reliquaries of my dead saint, and dwell
In the sweet odor of her memory.
Then in the uncouth solitude unlock
My stock of art, plant dials in the grass,
Hang in the air a bright thermometer
And aim a telescope at the inviolate sun.

CHARDON ST., BOSTON, 1831.

Day by day returns
The everlasting sun,
Replenishing material urns
With God's unspared donation;

But the day of day,
The orb within the mind,
Creating fair and good alway,
Shines not as once it shined.
* * *

Vast the realm of Being is,
In the waste one nook is his;
Whatsoever hap befalls
In his vision's narrow walls
He is here to testify.
1831.

HYMN

There is in all the sons of men
A love that in the spirit dwells,
That panteth after things unseen,
And tidings of the future tells.

And God hath built his altar here
To keep this fire of faith alive,
And sent his priests in holy fear
To speak the truth—for truth to strive.

And hither come the pensive train
Of rich and poor, of young and old,
Of ardent youth untouched by pain,
Of thoughtful maids and manhood bold.

They seek a friend to speak the word
Already trembling on their tongue,
To touch with prophet's hand the chord
Which God in human hearts hath strung.

To speak the plain reproof of sin
That sounded in the soul before,
And bid you let the angels in
That knock at meek contrition's door.

A friend to lift the curtain up
That hides from man the mortal goal,
And with glad thoughts of faith and hope
Surprise the exulting soul.

Sole source of light and hope assured,
O touch thy servant's lips with power,
So shall he speak to us the word
Thyself dost give forever more.
June, 1831.

SELF-RELIANCE

Henceforth, please God, forever I forego
The yoke of men's opinions. I will be
Light-hearted as a bird, and live with God.
I find him in the bottom of my heart,
I hear continually his voice therein.
* * *

The little needle always knows the North,
The little bird remembereth his note,
And this wise Seer within me never errs.
I never taught it what it teaches me;
I only follow, when I act aright.

October 9, 1832.

And when I am entombed in my place,
Be it remembered of a single man,
He never, though he dearly loved his race,
For fear of human eyes swerved from his plan.

Oh what is Heaven but the fellowship
Of minds that each can stand against the world
By its own meek and incorruptible will?

The days pass over me
And I am still the same;
The aroma of my life is gone
With the flower with which it came.
1833.

WRITTEN IN NAPLES

We are what we are made; each following day
Is the Creator of our human mould
Not less than was the first; the all-wise God
Gilds a few points in every several life,
And as each flower upon the fresh hillside,
And every colored petal of each flower,
Is sketched and dyed, each with a new design,
Its spot of purple, and its streak of brown,
So each man's life shall have its proper lights,
And a few joys, a few peculiar charms,
For him round in the melancholy hours
And reconcile him to the common days.
Not many men see beauty in the fogs
Of close low pine-woods in a river town;
Yet unto me not morn's magnificence,
Nor the red rainbow of a summer eve,
Nor Rome, nor joyful Paris, nor the halls
Of rich men blazing hospitable light,
Nor wit, nor eloquence,—no, nor even the song
Of any woman that is now alive,—
Hath such a soul, such divine influence,
Such resurrection of the happy past,
As is to me when I behold the morn
Ope in such law moist roadside, and beneath
Peep the blue violets out of the black loam,
Pathetic silent poets that sing to me
Thine elegy, sweet singer, sainted wife.
March, 1833.

WRITTEN AT ROME

Alone in Rome. Why, Rome is lonely too;—
Besides, you need not be alone; the soul
Shall have society of its own rank.
Be great, be true, and all the Scipios,
The Catos, the wise patriots of Rome,
Shall flock to you and tarry by your side,
And comfort you with their high company.
Virtue alone is sweet society,
It keeps the key to all heroic hearts,
And opens you a welcome in them all.
You must be like them if you desire them,
Scorn trifles and embrace a better aim
Than wine or sleep or praise;
Hunt knowledge as the lover wooes a maid,
And ever in the strife of your own thoughts
Obey the nobler impulse; that is Rome:
That shall command a senate to your side;
For there is no might in the universe
That can contend with love. It reigns forever.
Wait then, sad friend, wait in majestic peace
The hour of heaven. Generously trust
Thy fortune's web to the beneficent hand
That until now has put his world in fee
To thee. He watches for thee still. His love
Broods over thee, and as God lives in heaven,
However long thou walkest solitary,
The hour of heaven shall come, the man appear.
1833.

WEBSTER

1831

Let Webster's lofty face
Ever on thousands shine,
A beacon set that Freedom's race
Might gather omens from that radiant sign.

FROM THE PHI BETA KAPPA POEM

1834

Ill fits the abstemious Muse a crown to weave
For living brows; ill fits them to receive:
And yet, if virtue abrogate the law,
One portrait—fact or fancy—we may draw;
A form which Nature cast in the heroic mould
Of them who rescued liberty of old;
He, when the rising storm of party roared,
Brought his great forehead to the council board,
There, while hot heads perplexed with fears the state,
Calm as the morn the manly patriot sate;
Seemed, when at last his clarion accents broke,
As if the conscience of the country spoke.
Not on its base Monadnoc surer stood,
Than he to common sense and common good:
No mimic; from his breast his counsel drew,
Believed the eloquent was aye the true;
He bridged the gulf from th' alway good and wise
To that within the vision of small eyes.
Self-centred; when he launched the genuine word
It shook or captivated all who heard,
Ran from his mouth to mountains and the sea,
And burned in noble hearts proverb and prophecy.
1854

Why did all manly gifts in Webster fail?
He wrote on Nature's grandest brow, *For Sale*.

INDEX OF FIRST LINES

Atom from atom yawns as far

    Be of good cheer, brave spirit; steadfastly

Because I was content with these poor fields

Bethink, poor heart, what bitter kind of jest

Blooms the laurel which belongs

Boon Nature yields each day a brag which we now first behold

Bring me wine, but wine which never grew

Bulkeley, Hunt, Willard, Hosmer, Meriam, Flint

Burly, dozing humble-bee

But God said

But if thou do thy best

But Nature whistled with all her winds

But never yet the man was found

But over all his crowning grace

By fate, not option, frugal Nature gave

By the rude bridge that arched the flood

By thoughts I lead

    Can rules or tutors educate

Cast the bantling on the rocks

Coin the day dawn into lines

    Dark flower of Cheshire garden

Darlings of children and of bard

Daughter of Heaven and Earth, coy Spring

Daughters of Time, the hypocritic Days

Day by day for her darlings to her much she added more

Day by day returns

Day! hast thou two faces

Dear brother, would you know the life

Dearest, where thy shadow falls

Deep in the man sits fast his fate

Each spot where tulips prank their state
Each the herald is who wrote
Easy to match what others do
Ere he was born, the stars of fate
Ever the Poet *from* the land
Ever the Rock of Ages melts
Every day brings a ship
Every thought is public

Fall, stream, from Heaven to bless; return as well
Farewell, ye lofty spires
Flow, flow the waves hated
For art, for music over-thrilled
For every God
For Fancy's gift
For Genius made his cabin wide
For joy and beauty planted it
For Nature, true and like in every place
For thought, and not praise
For what need I of book or priest
Forbore the ant-hill, shunned to tread
Freedom all winged expands
Friends to me are frozen wine
From fall to spring, the russet acorn
From high to higher forces
From the stores of eldest matter
From thy worth and weight the stars gravitate

Gifts of one who loved me
Give all to love
Give me truths
Give to barrows, trays and pans

Go if thou wilt, ambrosial flower

Go speed the stars of Thought

Go thou to thy learned task

Gold and iron are good

Good-bye, proud world! I'm going home

Grace, Beauty and Caprice

Gravely it broods apart on joy

Hark what, now loud, now low, the pining flute complains

Hast thou named all the birds without a gun?

Have ye seen the caterpillar

He could condense cerulean ether

He lives not who can refuse me

He planted where the deluge ploughed

He took the color of his vest

He who has a thousand friends has not a friend to spare

He who has no hands

Hear what British Merlin sung

Henceforth, please God, forever I forego

Her passions the shy violet

Her planted eye to-day controls

High was her heart, and yet was well inclined

Him strong Genius urged to roam

His instant thought a poet spoke

His tongue was framed to music

Hold of the Maker, not the Made

How much, preventing God, how much I owe

I, Alphonso, live and learn

I am not poor but I am proud

I am not wiser for my age

I am the Muse who sung alway

I bear in youth and sad infirmities

I cannot spare water or wine

I do not count the hours I spend

I framed his tongue to music

I grieve that better souls than mine

I have an arrow that will find its mark

I have no brothers and no peers

I have trod this path a hundred times

I heard or seemed to hear the chiding Sea

I hung my verses in the wind

I left my dreary page and sallied forth

I like a church; I like a cowl

I love thy music, mellow bell

I mourn upon this battle-field

I rake no coffined clay, nor publish wide

I reached the middle of the mount

I said to heaven that glowed above

I see all human wits

I serve you not, if you I follow

If bright the sun, he tarries

If curses be the wage of love

If I could put my woods in song

If my darling should depart

If the red slayer think he slays

Ill fits the abstemious Muse a crown to weave

Illusions like the tints of pearl

Illusion works impenetrable

In an age of fops and toys

In countless upward-striving waves

In Farsistan the violet spreads

In many forms we try

In May, when sea-winds pierced our solitudes

In my garden three ways meet

In the chamber, on the stairs

In the deep heart of man a poet dwells

In the suburb, in the town

In the turbulent beauty

In Walden wood the chickadee

It fell in the ancient periods

It is time to be old

Knows he who tills this lonely field

Let me go where'er I will

Let Webster's lofty face

Like vaulters in a circus round

Little thinks, in the field, yon red-cloaked clown

Long I followed happy guides

Love asks nought his brother cannot give

Love on his errand bound to go

Love scatters oil

Low and mournful be the strain

Man was made of social earth

Many things the garden shows

May be true what I had heard

Mine and yours

Mine are the night and morning

Mortal mixed of middle clay

Nature centres into balls

Never did sculptor's dream unfold

Night-dreams trace on Memory's wall

No fate, save by the victim's fault, is low

Not in their houses stand the stars

October woods wherein
O fair and stately maid, whose eyes
O pity that I pause!
O tenderly the haughty day
O well for the fortunate soul
O what are heroes, prophets, men
Of all wit's uses the main one
Of Merlin wise I learned a song
Oh what is Heaven but the fellowship
On a mound an Arab lay
On bravely through the sunshine and the showers
On prince or bride no diamond stone
On two days it steads not to run from thy grave
Once I wished I might rehearse
One musician is sure
Our eyeless bark sails free
Over his head were the maple buds

Pale genius roves alone
Parks and ponds are good by day
Philosophers are lined with eyes within
Power that by obedience grows
Put in, drive home the sightless wedges

Quit the hut, frequent the palace

Right upward on the road of fame
Roomy Eternity
Roving, roving, as it seems
Ruby wine is drunk by knaves

Samson stark at Dagon's knee

See yonder leafless trees against the sky

Seek not the spirit, if it hide

Seems, though the soft sheen all enchants

Set not thy foot on graves

She is gamesome and good

She paints with white and red the moors

She walked in flowers around my field

Shines the last age, the next with hope is seen

Shun passion, fold the hands of thrift

Six thankful weeks,—and let it be

Slighted Minerva's learnèd tongue

Soft and softlier hold me, friends!

Solar insect on the wing

Some of your hurts you have cured

Space is ample, east and west

Spin the ball! I reel, I burn

Such another peerless queen

Sudden gusts came full of meaning

Tell me, maiden, dost thou use

Tell men what they knew before

Test of the poet is knowledge of love

Thanks to the morning light

That book is good

That each should in his house abide

That you are fair or wise is vain

The April winds are magical

The archangel Hope

The Asmodean feat is mine

The atom displaces all atoms beside

The bard and mystic held me for their own

The beggar begs by God's command

The brave Empedocles, defying fools

The brook sings on, but sings in vain

The cold gray down upon the quinces lieth

The cup of life is not so shallow

The days pass over me

The debt is paid

The gale that wrecked you on the sand

The green grass is bowing

The heavy blue chain

The living Heaven thy prayers respect

The lords of life, the lords of life

The low December vault in June be lifted high

Theme no poet gladly sung

The mountain and the squirrel

The Muse's hill by Fear is guarded

The patient Pan

The prosperous and beautiful

The rhyme of the poet

The rocky nook with hilltops three

The rules to men made evident

The sea is the road of the bold

The sense of the world is short

The solid, solid universe

The South-wind brings

The Sphinx is drowsy

The sun athwart the cloud thought it no sin

The sun goes down, and with him takes

The sun set, but set not his hope

The tongue is prone to lose the way

The water understands

The wings of Time are black and white

The word of the Lord by night

The yesterday doth never smile

Thee, dear friend, a brother soothes

There are beggars in Iran and Araby

There is in all the sons of men

There is no great and no small

There is no architect

They brought me rubies from the mine

They put their finger on their lips

They say, through patience, chalk

Thine eyes still shined for me, though far

Think me not unkind and rude

This is he, who, felled by foes

This shining moment is an edifice

Thou foolish Hafiz! Say, do churls

Thou shalt make thy house

Though her eyes seek other forms

Though loath to grieve

Though love repine and reason chafe

Thousand minstrels woke within me

Thy foes to hunt, thy enviers to strike down

Thy summer voice, Musketaquit

Thy trivial harp will never please

To and fro the Genius flies

To clothe the fiery thought

To transmute crime to wisdom, so to stem

Trees in groves

True Brahmin, in the morning meadows wet

Try the might the Muse affords

Two things thou shalt not long for, if thou love a mind serene

Two well-assorted travellers use

Unbar the door, since thou the Opener art

Venus, when her son was lost

Was never form and never face

We are what we are made; each following day

We crossed Champlain to Keeseville with our friends

We love the venerable house

Well and wisely said the Greek

What all the books of ages paint, I have

What care I, so they stand the same

What central flowing forces, say

When all their blooms the meadows flaunt

When I was born

When success exalts thy lot

When the pine tosses its cones

When wrath and terror changed Jove's regal port

Who gave thee, O Beauty

Who knows this or that? 375.

Who saw the hid beginnings

Who shall tell what did befall

Why did all manly gifts in Webster fail?

Why fear to die

Why lingerest thou, pale violet, to see the dying year

Why should I keep holiday

Wilt thou seal up the avenues of ill?

Winters know

Wise and polite, — and if I drew

Wisp and meteor nightly falling
With beams December planets dart
With the key of the secret he marches faster
Would you know what joy is hid

    Yes, sometimes to the sorrow-stricken
You shall not be overbold
You shall not love me for what daily spends
Your picture smiles as first it smiled

INDEX OF TITLES

[The titles in small capital letters are those of the principal divisions of the work; those in lower case are of single poems, or the subdivisions of long poems.]

QUATRAINS AND TRANSLATIONS